W9-BZO-040

The Listener

The Listener

In the Shadow of the Holocaust

Irene Oore

Printed and bound in Canada at Marquis. The text of this book is printed on 100% post-consumer recycled paper with earth-friendly vegetable-based inks.

The Uses Of Sorrow from *Thirst* by Mary Oliver, published by Beacon Press, Boston. Copyright © 2004 by Mary Oliver, used herewith by permission of the Charlotte Sheedy Literary Agency, Inc.

Cover photo: The author with her mother Stefa, 1953. Courtesy of the author.
Cover design: Duncan Campbell, University of Regina Press
Text design: John van der Woude, JVDW Designs
Copy editor: Marionne Cronin
Proofreader: Nadine Coderre

Library and Archives Canada Cataloguing in Publication

Title: The listener : in the shadow of the Holocaust / Irene Oore.
Names: Oore, Irène, 1948- author.
Series: Regina collection ; 13.
Description: Series statement: The Regina collection ; 13
Identifiers: Canadiana (print) 20190110058 | Canadiana (ebook) 20190110074 | ISBN 9780889776531 (hardcover) | ISBN 9780889776548 (PDF) | ISBN 9780889776555 (HTML)
Subjects: LCSH: Oore, Irène, 1948- | LCSH: Oore, Irène, 1948—Family. | LCSH: Knopf, Stefania. | LCSH: Children of Holocaust survivors—Poland—Biography. | LCSH: Holocaust, Jewish (1939-1945)—Poland—Biography. | LCSH: Jews—Poland—Biography. | LCSH: Poland—Biography. | LCSH: Autobiographies.
Classification: LCC DS134.72.O57 A3 2019 | DDC 940.53/18092—dc23

10 9 8 7 6 5 4 3 2

University of Regina Press, University of Regina
Regina, Saskatchewan, Canada, S4S 0A2
tel: (306) 585-4758 fax: (306) 585-4699
web: www.uofrpress.ca

We acknowledge the support of the Canada Council for the Arts for our publishing program. We acknowledge the financial support of the Government of Canada. / Nous reconnaissons l'appui financier du gouvernement du Canada. This publication was made possible with support from Creative Saskatchewan's Book Publishing Production Grant Program.

Canada Council   Conseil des Arts
for the Arts   du Canada

 Canada

 creative SASKATCHEWAN

*Dedicated to my four children, who have lived
all their lives in the shadow of this untold story.*

Contents

II

*Map of Poland, circa 1940, showing the General
Government territory of German-occupied Poland.*

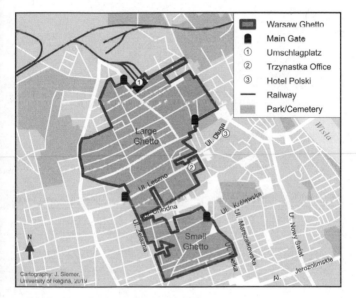

*Map of Warsaw Ghetto, where the Nazis
imprisoned Polish Jews from 1940 until 1943.*

This story is rising from her ashes and
from a deep and hollow place within me.

I

The Gift

S HE GAVE ME LIFE. SHE THEN OFFERED ME death, a daily ration of it. This life-then-death was a precious and wonderful gift; in fact, it was the only gift worth giving.

For years, I had resisted the gift. However, she never stopped offering it, seeing beyond my stubborn resistance and my overwhelming fear.

Her gift was a true offering: the possibility to witness suffering the way she had observed it, the opportunity to have a glimpse into a slice of her story, the way she recalled it.

A gift I could not refuse. Oh, I tried. I would not listen, blocking the words from penetrating my consciousness. I would shut my eyes and imagine being on the beach, on the Baltic. When the wind would blow, the grains of sand would hit me very hard on my face, on my body, all at once. Like her words. Wicker shelters with benches were dispersed on this northern beach. I would imagine hiding in one of those shelters. I would plead with her to stop; I would explain that I had already heard it.

Now I think that I could have tried, perhaps, telling her that I just was not able to bear the cruelty of it all. Now I wonder whether I could have, maybe, said to her that I was too little (she started 'gifting' me, the first time I recall, when I was perhaps four years old). I suppose I could have pointed out to her that it all happened before I was born, so I could not really relieve all that suffering. Because I thought it was my duty to relieve it. Her suffering and that of the others.

Yet, at the time, it did not occur to me to explain any of this to her. At the time I must have already felt, without being able to articulate it 'til much later, that I was responsible for what had happened. I now think that all those who belong to the human race were and are responsible for each crime committed. It did not occur to me 'til much, much later, that my listening to her, however imperfect, offered her perhaps a form of momentary relief. If it did, she never acknowledged it.

I was little, and she was relentless. She just kept on gifting. A daily gift of life and death. The death she carried in her belly. The death she carried in her soul. And her monumental and crushing resilience. The gift was tightly wrapped. It was hard and cold. Like a rock. The rock we traditionally place on the graves of those we loved and whom we miss.

When she exhaled for the very last time, when her final long breath was released into the silence which followed, it was yet another gift. The gift of life wrapped in the belly of death wrapped in the belly of life.

Perhaps she had said, "I will talk and tell you the story, and you must listen." She may have said, "I will talk 'til my breath is gone, 'til there is nothing left but ashes, the ashes of millions of children, women, and men—your ashes and mine. And you will listen."

Could she have said, "I will tell you what really happened; your duty is to listen." She could have added, "You will listen 'til I stop talking, because this is why you were born. You were born to listen to this story and to this story only. You were born in the belly of this story."

She could have added, with a characteristic mixture of righteousness and scorn, that there would be no silly fairy tales, no imaginary creatures, no talking trees, and no elves. No happy endings either. Just the unfolding horror of the gruesome story.

And I listened; I hardly ever dared ask her to please stop the telling, to please, please let me go to the safety of my doll corner, behind the cabinet, to please let me hide there quietly and sing soothing lullabies to the dolls, covering up with those tunes the harshness of the story which was echoing and reverberating in me, like an unwelcome guest.

The story that still echoes now, as I, an old woman (much older than she was when the telling began), am writing these words.

However, there was no hiding from the story. Even now there is no quiet shelter from it.

I was swallowed by this dark tale, and I would, over and over, hit my fists against the walls that enclosed me in the bloody belly of the leviathan.

There was no way out.

Longing

I REMEMBER MY OWN LONGING AS A CHILD FOR what had been lost to me before I was ever born. I was a lonely child, growing up between two 'survivors'— no, between four older Holocaust survivors: my mother, Stefa, and father, Marian, and my mother's sister, Flora, and her husband, Teo. All four were haunted by their past, every moment of every day and every moment of every night. I was their proof that they actually survived.

The only child for both couples, I was their link to the present and to the future. I was to exhibit joy and gratitude at all times and infuse these feelings into my beloved 'walking dead,' my own personal ghosts.

I was unable, as a child, to pinpoint what was missing from my life: grandparents, family, siblings, celebrations, rituals (except, of course, the ritual of retelling the story). What was missing was magic, the magic of fairy tales, the magic of possibility and of lightness; instead, I got my daily heaping portion of a hard, bony death story.

So when my parents took me for a visit to the Skull Chapel, I was not surprised. Horrified, but not surprised. I do not recall any other details of that visit. Just the skulls surrounding me. Looking at me with their hollow eyes from the ceiling and from the walls. These skulls were not Holocaust skulls but, in the mind of the six-year-old that I was, they had merged with all my mother's accounts. This visit somehow verified for me all the stories with which I had lived and which I wished in vain to be untrue.

Starvation—*Głód*

THEY WERE HUNGRY. THEY WERE COLD. EVERY second of every minute of every hour. When she and her sister, Flora, lived in a small room in an attic, next to a cemetery, they were so hungry and so cold that it was difficult to fall asleep. Their entire bodies, their whole beings, were screaming, begging for food and for warmth.

The room was icy and dark and one sister would whisper to the other, "When this is all over, I will invite you to my place, and I will offer you a thick slice of a white, sweet, fresh-from-the-oven *challah* bread with a generous layer of sweet butter on top. And to drink, I will prepare a steaming cup of hot cocoa…"

Her sister, having savoured this fleeting and aromatic dream of a feast, would reciprocate: "The following evening *I* will invite *you* over to my warm and cozy place. I will set up a table for the two of us. The table will be covered with a hand-embroidered festive tablecloth. Two porcelain, gold-trimmed plates, two elegant, gold-trimmed china mugs, beautifully shiny, freshly polished silver spoons, and embroidered napkins matching the tablecloth will be set on the table. I will serve you the thickest slice of bread you have ever seen, and on it I will spread freshly churned, sweet butter. In the porcelain mugs I will pour, slowly, the steaming, thick, rich, hot cocoa."

Neither she nor her sister could conjure up any other dream of a feast. It was the very same one every evening to rock them to a starving, cold, and frightened sleep.

She would tell me this as a bedtime story. I can still feel my immense hopelessness, my vast despair, as I listened to this ever-echoing story in which there were no fairies, there was no magic, and where even basic imagination was failing. And I was helpless and sad. And feeling guilty for having a full belly.

Another story of starvation, recounted numerous times, happened in *Warszawskie Getto* (Warsaw Ghetto). She was returning to her Ghetto apartment, which she shared with her mother and her sister and several others. She was excited: she was not coming home empty-handed. In her hand she held a trophy, a rare find, wrapped in a piece of newspaper. She had sold a hand-embroidered tablecloth. (Was it her mother's beautiful work? It never occurred to me to ask.) With the money she got, she managed to buy two fresh carrots from somewhere. She was returning home, to her mother and sister, with this colourful trophy.

And while a jubilatory voice of hope was singing inside her, "carrots, carrots, vitamins for my sister and my mother," she met an acquaintance. A fine man, a lawyer she had known in Łódź from before the war.

They greeted each other, exchanged a few words, inquired about each other's families. And all this time the man would not look her in the eyes. All this time he seemed fidgety. Sheepish. Then it happened. Suddenly, shockingly, in each retelling of the story. Without looking at her, the man grabbed one of the carrots and started running.

"He grabbed one of the carrots," she would repeat, years later, still bewildered. She would then conclude, in each retelling of the story, "Clearly he was hungrier than I was. Had he asked me, I would have given him both carrots. He could have had both."

The darkest starvation story was unconcealed many, many years later; she was in her nineties. Demented. Frontal lobe dementia. In many ways not resembling herself anymore.

She called me on the phone with this unexpected, late confession. Her voice was childlike, and it was filled with tears. "It was during the war," she explained. After she had managed to get her mother and her sister out of the Ghetto. After she herself had also managed to escape from the Warsaw Ghetto. After she had managed to place both mother and sister in hiding with a different Gentile family, each in a different city.

She herself worked on the 'Aryan side' (*po aryjskiej stronie*) and paid each of the two families to hide her mother and sister. When she had a day off she would travel from Warszawa to visit one or the other.

I knew all of that. She did not have to explain any of it. Perhaps she had forgotten that I knew. Perhaps she never remembered all the previous war story telling-sessions because it did not really matter how many times she had told them; she just felt the urge to tell them over and over again.

Perhaps she had decided a very long time ago that my listening was flawed and her retelling was inexorably pointless, and yet she felt it was absolutely essential. Otherwise she could have, in this last broken confession, gone straight to the heart of it.

That day she had travelled on the train from Warsaw to see her mother. In her handbag, wrapped in newspaper, she had an end of a loaf of bread. This piece of bread was for her mother. As she entered the house where her mother was hidden, she encountered the owners' little girl. The child was about six years old and, like everyone, she too was hungry. As she was telling me this my mother started crying; this old, old, broken woman who all her life, and even toward the end, hardly ever cried…

She confessed giving the piece of bread to the child. Taking it away from her own mother. "Perhaps *Mama* could have lived a bit longer had I given the bread to her that day?" she asked me in a pitiful, childlike voice.

I replied, firmly, "No": I now was my mother's mother. I said that her mama (*Twoja matka*) would not have lived any longer. I reminded her that her mother had died of a sick heart. As if it proved the bread would not have made a difference. But her reasoning was gone; she had no choice but to rely on mine.

And as I put down the phone, I cried. For my grand-mother, who died of heart failure a very short time after this episode, sick, hungry, and alone in her hiding, the woman I never met and whom, according to my mother, I resembled.

I cried for my mother, who had kept this secret for some sixty years, for all the secrets I was never going to hear, and for all those I had heard innumerable times, secrets which kept reverberating in me as in a dark and empty cave.

Shortly after her 'confession,' my mother passed away; in fact, she starved to death! She had been having what I referred to as 'drowning episodes.' Her swallowing reflex was failing and eating was provoking these episodes. She was suffering from aspirational pneumonia.

I witnessed, horrified, a few of those drownings. She was choking and making low, throaty, gurgling noises; it was unbearable. After one of those episodes, as I sat next to her, helplessly crying, she turned toward me and said clearly, in her lucid, undemented voice, "To *jest piekło*." ("*This* is hell.")

I went to talk to her doctor, checked what it all meant and what the options were. I spent days and nights struggling to wrap my mind around her situation, and then I knew.

And I told her. I hardly believe that I told her. I told her to stop eating. When I did, she turned toward me, asked "*Co?!*", meaning "What?!" Did she not hear? Did she not believe that I had said that? I could not believe that *I had* said that. And so I had to repeat it: "*Przestaj jeść!*" "Stop eating!"

It took her a few days to wrap her demented and broken mind around her situation and around my advice. Which was true to her nature: my mother liked to think things through, slowly, carefully, deliberately.

Then she stopped eating. Entirely. In an ironic twist of fate, my mother ended up choosing starvation as her way to die, as her way to freedom from an unbearable life. Starvation finally became her ally.

The Promise

SHE ENTRUSTED ME WITH THE STORY. SHE refused to tell it to the Spielberg Foundation people, she refused to tell it to *byle kto* (just anyone). I was not just anyone; I was her only daughter, the chosen one.

Wasn't I the one who had heard fragments of the story, on a daily basis, for decades? Wasn't I regularly accused of not listening carefully enough, of being too distracted, of daydreaming? (And daydream I did—of having been adopted, of living an entirely different life with a different family: daydreams which were my secret and which my parents would have been horrified to discover.)

Wasn't I allowed, a few years before she died, to write down the story as she retold it once again? And then, a few weeks after I had it down, one evening, wasn't I the one she telephoned? She had thought about it all, she said. She gave me permission to modify details; she insisted that names had to be changed to protect the identity of all those involved, as well as their children and grandchildren.

She was letting go; the story was now truly in my possession. The understanding was that I would tell the story. That was the deal: the story was now mine, and I had the moral obligation to tell it.

The story had lived in me, had grown in me, had filled every nook of my being, and the time was right. It was time to look at the story and acknowledge my immense debt to it, my gratitude. For without it, I would not be who I am, in the most intimate way; without it, my relationship to good and evil would not be the same; my relationship to beauty, and the drunken intensity accompanying it, would not be the same. I owe my life to this story. To reclaim my life, the story had to be told.

So why, for years, even after her death, was there the monumental, overwhelming fear? Why the conviction that telling it would actually engulf me in an abyss? Was I awed by its sacredness? Was I simply afraid that I was not equal to the task? Was it the belief that, not having suffered enough, I did not deserve to tell this story? Or was it the horror, the poisonous evil in it, that I was terrified would burn through me as I retold it? Was I perhaps unsure about my own interpretation of it? Would I really be able to distinguish her story and interpretation from my own?

These scruples and a general anxiety surrounding the story were, and still are, disturbingly present for me.

However, as scared as I am, I will tell the story. For what was "If I tell the story, I will die," has transformed into "If I stay silent, I will not ever be really alive"; as Jonah, I must have arrived at the shores of my Nineveh.

The Double Bind

I T HAS LIVED INSIDE ME FOR MOST OF MY LIFE. It weighed so much that I could never run or laugh or even speak without it rattling in me like a chained skeleton. I thought that no one heard it rattle but me. Now I am convinced that many sensed the rattling, though perhaps had no idea what it was. I sometimes wonder what they thought they had heard. It was unspeakable. And I truly could not speak of it. I was sure that I was incapable of it. That I had no right. That I had not suffered enough. That mine was merely ersatz suffering. It was a second-hand suffering. Hers, stoic and righteous, was the only real one. Her daily Holocaust gift to me. It was a great privilege she thought, and I agreed, and I felt unworthy of it.

It started when I was a small child. Each day came with its story. She sent me, most reluctantly, to daycare for one day only. I enjoyed myself, loved the company of all the other children, and liked the food. I hated naptime, though. That constituted enough of a 'reason'—a pretext; she decided that I would not go to daycare. Instead I would stay at home with her. I suppose she felt that this way she would have more time to tell me, that I could hear more.

In all fairness, she did not know whether she would live long enough; she had to hurry, she was in a race with cancer. Diagnosed with cancer when I was two years old, my mother ended up surviving this death call as well.

The stories were about bombs and terror, about Nazi and Ukrainian soldiers, about Jews and Poles and shelters and fear. Stories of the Star of David patches and of the Warsaw Ghetto. Shame, humiliation, and hunger stories. The obsessive descriptions of the typical look of a Jew. The scared eyes. She truly believed she had the ability to tell a Jew apart from a non-Jew. She spoke of the Aryan 'good' look she was fortunate to have. She told me stories of typhoid fever, of betrayals and denunciations. I listened. Fascinated and terrorized. A small child, then a pre-adolescent, a teenager. Daily.

She was satisfying a need in herself as well as what she considered her sacred duty. She was bearing witness. I wanted to unburden her. I wanted to take on her suffering.

Yet, no matter how intently I listened to her, she disapproved. She complained that deep down I did not 'really'

want to hear. There was truth in that. Her pain and suffering behind a pretense of rational discourse were infinite. I
was listening to the sensible story covering up her unbearable horror and her deep panic.

Her stories, she believed, had an 'educational' point;
there was a moral lesson. These were cautionary tales; this
terror, this hatred, this systematic extermination, all of
these—she would conclude repeatedly—were manifesta-
tions of human nature. This was what one human being
was capable of doing to another human being.

"This," she would tell the child sitting in front of her,
"is what you and I carry inside us, this potential for hatred
and murder. Jews and Poles, Austrians and Germans, and
everyone else, all alike."

I knew her despair: cold and boundless. I felt that, perhaps, my suffering could compensate for not having lived
through this hell myself. Obviously, it was not the same as
having lived through it, I thought, but it was all I could do.

She never gave me any advice or instructions as to how
exactly she wished for me to listen. She had no words of
wisdom as to how a child, later a teenager, was to process
this. Surely if she could live through this, I could find a
way to hear it. Yet she was dissatisfied and irritated with
my listening. Over and over again, I failed her.

Only recently did it occur to me that all those years,
under the mask of a rational, reasonable, and collected person, the person I knew as my mother, lived a madwoman,
so deeply scarred that she was unrecognizable even to

herself. The persona she presented to me was inhibited and inhibiting, highly judgmental of my doomed efforts.

She appeared confident that her judgment was infallible. Underneath that mask there was fear, hurt, anger, and rage. Underneath, there was a feeling of abandonment and of betrayal, of defensiveness and of guilt. Underneath, there was a sense of an interrupted, broken life, of madness and fury.

Yet I miss my mother achingly. I miss the mother I could have had and whom I lost before I was born. I miss the leftover mother I had. She was still grand. I miss her loyalty, her fierce love, her rigour, her irony, and above all her steadiness. I miss her the way she could have been and the way she was.

Death Womb

URING THE WAR, MANY WOMEN STOPPED menstruating. My mother did. When on the Aryan side, she consulted a gynecologist; he told her that her uterus had shrunk to the size of a string.

The only brother I had, had died in her womb. She gave birth to him on December 6, 1945, two and a half years before I was born. It was a stillbirth. What was his death date? She named him Piotr and called him Piotruś. Peter, Petros, stone, rock. She talked about him with great tenderness.

I often wondered what it would have been like to have had a brother. He was born after the Holocaust, and his dead, macerated little body had inhabited the same womb in which my journey started.

Two years after my birth, the same space was inhabited briefly by another potential baby and, simultaneously, by cancer.

Womb, fetus, and cancer had to all be excised (I had always sensed that the womb where my life began was a space of death), had to be cut out, and any remaining cells of it to be bombarded with radiation and to be destroyed.

It occurred to me that my siblings-to-be were killed by the story. I imagined my mother's body expelling death, then me, then death again. I have never been a true only child; rather, I have been a middle child between two dead siblings.

Alchemy

PIOTR WAS MEANT TO BE THE LISTENER. HE died just a short while before being born. Perhaps he sensed in some mysterious way the kind of story for which he was destined, and he just could not face it.

So I was born to listen to it. I thought that I was born to absorb as much of it as I could. To lighten her burden. Now, I think that this was not the appropriate way of unburdening her. I am not sure what kind of listening would have been appropriate for a child. I suppose *appropriate* is not the right word, and I wonder what is the right word or whether the right word even exists.

In order to muster the courage to continue living and listening, I had to believe that I could actually help, that the stories, and the suffering which was at their very core, could—through some alchemy—be transformed into beauty and praise. Her despair was bottomless; she had no God and she saw humans, with some rare exceptions, as monsters; she viewed humanity's history as a long chain of the transmission of violence; she was sternly sad and profoundly hurt.

I was too young to articulate this; however, I felt that my role on this earth was to lift her spirits as much and as frequently as I could.

I remember myself as a child trying very hard to keep my parents (as well as my aunt and her husband) smiling or, at the very least, not as obviously distraught. I would recite poems, be clever, ask smart questions, be silly and cute, just to entertain the four of them. For the child I was, and later for the adult I grew into, it was to be a life-long Sisyphean undertaking. To infuse joy into darkness, to infuse lightness into weightiness, to infuse hope into despair was my task on this earth. Looking back, I see myself as a sad child-harlequin.

I was a child who had the responsibility—no, the mission—to work very hard to keep four ghosts attached to life.

Voices

WHEN I BECAME A TEENAGER AND CAME into my voiceprint, people would remark that it was similar to my mother's. We sounded the same; they would confuse us when we answered the phone. My mother has gifted me not only with her story but also with her voice! She passed away, and now the story and the voice live in me, and I hear my *matka* from within. The two voices, hers and mine, combine, echo one another, sometimes struggle and separate, only to combine once again. Inextricable yet distinct voices: hers and mine.

Words

I WILL PLACE ONE WORD, BIG AND STRONG, THEN on top of it another one, and yet another, 'til I reach my destination.

I will roll my word like a huge boulder into the ocean, and then another one, 'til the water rises.

I will just keep on writing. One word in front of the other. One word at a time. I will write in English, my most 'foreign' language. I love the familiar strangeness of its words, these words which offer me the freedom one has in a foreign territory, a territory where one does not know the rules and can therefore pretend that there are none.

I will write in English, the language of my children, for they may wish to discover the story of the story. Her story, inside which I was born. The labyrinths of words and feelings, with no golden thread, no *fil d'Ariane* to help me find my way. No golden thread either for my children to find their way to light. This story as a small monument on the grave where her ashes are interred. So that finally gratitude and joy may be possible?

II

Her Story: The Beginning

S HE AND I SIT IN HER APARTMENT, IN A DINING nook off the kitchen. It is small and sheltered from the world. We sit next to each other; she is on my left. Every day we sit at the same table, on the same chairs. For three or four hours at a time we sit at her hexagonal glass table. In order to protect the glass she had made a special red felt cover that fits the table and is attached to it with sewn-in elastics.

I have a pad of graph paper in front of me and a pen in my hand. I come every day for weeks, and I write down her words while she talks. She speaks in Polish and I translate immediately into English. She is in her late eighties. Her voice is clear (she kept that young voice 'til her fall, 'til she was ninety-two. I can still hear her).

"September 1, 1939; first bombing of Łódź. I was sick with terror."

She says this in her everyday, matter-of-fact voice. That normal, down-to-earth voice to describe the horror and atrocity is uniquely hers; the tension between the sound and the meaning it conveys, enormous. Oh my God, I never thought I could miss that, but now, years after her death, I do.

"Young German people, *Volksdeutsche*, marching through Łódź, singing German marching songs. Jews are scared to go outside. The front doors to cafés, restaurants, and other public places display a sign: *Żydom i psom wstęp wzbroniony.*"

Entrance forbidden to Jews and dogs.

"People line up to buy food. If a Jew stands in the line-up, he gets pushed out by Poles and Germans." (She is offering me humiliation. The humiliation she somehow, in a twisted sort of way, appears to justify.)

"Łódź is now part of the Reich. It is getting colder. Fall is advancing. A new order: Jews are to make for themselves a distinct, yellow Star of David, a ten-centimetre patch (*łata*), and they are to wear it on the front and on the back, just below the left shoulder blade, where the heart is. The Germans ask for the most visible, the brightest yellow, so that anyone can easily recognize a Jew, spit on him, or shoot him from a distance. Anyone can pick Jews off the street and order them to work.

"I had a beautiful black coat, and as I was sewing the yellow patch on it, I was crying; now anyone who wished to do so could spit on me, anyone could take me to work, and they could be rewarded for it." (She states this as if it is completely obvious.)

She says that she cried when crocheting and sewing, but she does not cry when she is telling me this. I am grateful. Her very rare tears always panicked me. I felt responsible for them: Did I in any way cause them? Did I fail to prevent them?

And she reiterates, "The patch was so visible, so bright, anyone could spit on you, any time." (Could I have dared to ask, "Has anyone ever spit on you?" I was too scared of the answer. "Spit": in Polish, *pluć*.)

"Those Jews who are not strong enough to do the work demanded of them are beaten. They come to Jewish homes and take Jews away. Once, three Gestapo officers came to our house to search for money and, more specifically, for gold. My mother, a dental surgeon, had been allowed to keep gold in her cabinet. They took the loot and left.

"My mother, Sonia, my sister, Flora, and I decided to move to Warszawa (a larger city than Łódź, and at the time still part of Poland, so, we thought, perhaps safer), but those who wore the yellow Star of David were not allowed to purchase train tickets. I covered my yellow patch with a fur shawl and bought the tickets. We packed many suitcases. In them we stuffed everything we could. We each took two suitcases with us to Warszawa. The other suitcases, which were to be sent to us, were stolen by the Polish maid and her brother or cousin.

•

"We arrived in Warszawa around Christmas of 1939. There was no wood or coal to be found, and that winter was a particularly bitter one. First we stayed with a lady with whom Flora had worked." My mother's sister was also a dentist. "Then we found Hala L., Flora's friend; Hala's parents' apartment building had been bombed, so she and her family moved to an apartment at Wielka 5. They let us sublet a room.

"In Warszawa, Jews wore a white arm band with a blue *Gwiazda Dawida*. Jews were to buy it; somehow, it felt less humiliating than the yellow patch."

I never asked her what she meant by this. Was it the band rather than the patch? Was it the arm rather than the heart? Was it the colour? Was it the fact that it was bought rather than self-made? Or perhaps just the fact that it was the second time around and that she got somewhat desensitized? I now wonder whether, in 1939, my mother had heard the story of David and Goliath, or whether the blue Star of David became more acceptable only in retrospect as it became clearly associated with the Israeli flag. In Hebrew the Star of David is called *Magen David*, which translates as shield of David: a symbol of protection.

"The terror. On the streets. Jews were caught and taken to work. There was a curfew (*godzina policyjna*) when people were not allowed on the street past that hour. *Anyone* on the street could be shot. One evening the curfew hour passed and Hala's sister had not yet returned home. We found out later that she had been picked up to wash windows and floors....Another day, we were walking on the street and Niusia P.'s brother, Mietek L., was arrested; they wanted him to do some labour. But I said to the German officer, who seemed to like me, who seemed to think I was pretty, 'No! This is my brother!', and he replied, 'Quickly, go home with your *bruder*.'"

Did she remember the officer's face when she told the story? I felt guilty for having the trivial thought; did it really matter? Did any of my thoughts matter? I didn't think so.

That was the beginning of the last retelling of the story.

The deep humiliation of the bright yellow Star of David, the patch to be worn where the heart was, the spitting, the signs forbidding Jews and dogs to enter, have never left us. The shame and indignity associated with being Jewish never disappeared. Not even in Israel.

Both my mother and I woke up into this humiliation every morning.

⋯⋯⋯

Her story and mine: inextricably entangled. We sat beside each other. She talked, and I listened and wrote. I hardly dared look at her. She was little and frail, and she was old. This was the first time I had actually asked her to tell me the story.

I asked to be told; I came over to her apartment to be told. We were both a little frightened. What if it became completely unbearable for her to tell and for me to listen? This was her telling at what I considered her very best: no grand eloquence, no pathos, no drama.

Bomb Shelters

"WITH THE FIRST BOMBINGS IN ŁÓDŹ I RAN down to shelters like everyone else. Those shelters were stone cellars (*piwnice*) under the houses. And then I saw the dismembered, beheaded bodies of those who were buried under the rubble, the severed limbs, the disfigured faces, and never again did I go to a *piwnica* during a bombing."

The first day of the Yom Kippur War in 1973 in Israel. Yom Kippur in Israel is a profoundly silent day. No buses, no trains, no cars, no radio, no TV. A special kind of silence and a feeling of peace used to characterize this High Holiday.

That Yom Kippur, I had put down the baby for his nap. Then it happened: a loud, prolonged wailing of the siren.

A sense of cold horror. Israel had been attacked on the holiest holiday of all, the Day of Atonement.

I grabbed the baby from his crib and hurried down the stairs to the bomb shelter. All the neighbours were already gathered there. One of them had a little transistor radio and was trying to get some news. First there was nothing except some static crackling on the Israeli channels, as was always the case on Yom Kippur (on Galey Tsahal, the army channel), then some music came on: marches, funeral marches.

The feeling of horror was deepening. It was in my heart, in my stomach, in my guts. The siren kept wailing. Ten minutes into it, my mother and father, who lived nearby, arrived at our bomb shelter. My mother had with her some blended warm soup for my baby son, and she was furious; she said that she knew I would wake the baby up for no reason—then she rephrased, unnecessarily. She handed me the soup, saying she was certain that I would forget his soup, and she left the shelter followed by my father, who did not utter a word.

At the time it did not occur to me that, behind the anger and the scorn, there was terror. She had walked over to our house, then back to hers, while people were not supposed to be on the streets as they were expected to be in the bomb shelters.

Years later, when she told me again about the bodies pulled out from under the rubble, it occurred to me that, on that first day of the Yom Kippur War, she was not

calmer or more 'in control' than anyone else. She most
certainly was not more rational or lucid than the rest of
us (even though I may have thought so at the time). She
was simply getting back into a full-swing 'Holocaust sur-
vivor mode,' and she had absolutely no say in the matter. I
understood this only when she explained once again, with
her I-am-infinitely-patient-with-you voice and with the
firm conviction of being more rational than most, why
she never went back to a bomb shelter, having witnessed
scattered body parts after an apartment building took a
direct hit.

The Train

"OH! DID I MENTION THIS: ON THE TRAIN, JEWS were not allowed in the cars. We had to stand in the area linking them. We stood there, my sister Flora and I, with our old mother, on the train from Łódź to Warszawa. It was freezing. A few months before the war started, my mother had had a stroke, and she was still weak and wobbly."

Those gangways, those corridors connecting cars where children choose to stand waiting to be thrown off balance only to enjoy the recovery; here the entire world was off balance, and there was no recovery in sight.

Before the Warsaw Ghetto

"WHEN WE—MY MOTHER, SONIA, MY SISTER, Flora, and I—first arrived in Warszawa at the end of December of 1939, *Warszawskie Getto* did not yet exist. It was a particularly harsh winter in Poland. We were very cold most of the time.

"We lived at Wielka 5 for an entire year. My mother, my sister, and I all stayed in one room, and Hala and her entire family—her parents, her sister, her brother and his wife—all lived in the same apartment at Wielka 5."

I never asked her how many rooms there were in the Wielka apartment. I never asked how it was to live there, all nine of them. All but three of them —Hala, Flora, and my mother—were going to die within the following two to three years.

Why did I not ask about the friendships, alliances, tensions? Was it the fear that the unbearable story would digress and get even longer? She had been right all along in accusing me of not wanting to listen. I was not brave enough to hear what they had all endured (minute after minute, hour after hour, year after year). Was I using my vulnerability as a shield?

Many years later, in Tel Aviv, my mother, Stefa, her sister, Flora, and their friend, Hala, would meet every Friday afternoon in a café. With them, at the table, sat all their dead ones, parents and siblings, along with their grief and the incurable hurt which hardly ever left them. I sometimes sat with them too. I always wondered how they managed to squeeze around such a crowded café table and have a seemingly normal Friday-afternoon-coffee-place conversation.

I remember one time we were seated at Café Kapulski on Allenby Street when I saw a close friend of mine, Tammy S., with her mother. They were sitting at a neighbouring table. Both mother and daughter had been born in Israel. And I felt a sharp pang of envy. I imagined (wrongly?) that their café conversation was so much simpler, so much lighter, without having to share the table with the Holocaust skeletons, rattling, pushing each other, and tapping on the table with their bony phalanges.

"The winter of 1940 was bitterly cold."

That is all she told me of that entire winter. She knew that worse things were coming.

Getto Warszawskie, październik 1940
(Warsaw Ghetto, October 1940)

"THE GERMANS ANNOUNCED THE ESTABLISH-
ment of the Getto in Warszawa. They indicated
which Warszawa streets constituted it. Those streets
were shut off by fences. All Jews were ordered to move
into the Getto. German police and Ukrainian soldiers
guarded the fences. While some of the Germans appeared
to just be doing their 'job,' the Ukrainian soldiers seemed
to have a real calling. They were cruel and fierce, and they
hated the Jews. Their black uniforms terrified me."

Her voice is steady, her eyes are dry, and I am ever so
grateful to her for keeping her emotions in check.

"Nothing grew in the Warszawskie Getto. There were no trees, no grass, no flowers. It was divided into two parts, the large Getto and the small one. The two were connected by a bridge on Żelazna Street. In order to go from one part of the Getto to the other, one had to cross that bridge. The Jews crossing the bridge were to take off their hats when passing in front of the German policemen. It was quite devious as the Orthodox Jews are not to take off their hats; it is a sign of disrespect to God. Requiring people to take off their hats was humiliating for all Jews and gave the Germans a pretext to clobber the Orthodox Jews over the head. The policemen used rubber clubs."

These Orthodox Jews, in their stubborn belief, would keep their hats on and respect the very God who, according to their own logic, allowed all of this to happen. Her lack of understanding of those Jews, her extreme frustration with them, and her contradictory sadness and contempt—her voice and mine, her voice through mine. Perhaps if I retell the story in which I am still trapped I will miraculously get past her hurt and mine, perhaps I will even get past her contempt, which I carry in me.

It occurred to me that it could have seemed to some as if God, if there ever was one, was on the side of the Nazis.

In any case, the Orthodox Jews were hit over the head, and my mother, then, and I, ever since she told me, were angry with the Jews for keeping their hats on, for being clobbered over their heads. We were angry with them for

their choice, which we could not comprehend, angry with
them for being willing to suffer for those beliefs we did
not share, angry and terribly sad and helpless when con-
templating their stubborn faith.

It seems to me that the Germans and the Orthodox
Jews understood each others' positions perfectly well; the
victimizers and the victims both obeying the rules of a
desperately cruel and hopelessly predictable choreography.

"The Getto was conceived so that there was no way to
avoid certain streets, you just had to take them."

She is enumerating the names of the streets which
could not be avoided; she seems to possess a map in her
mind, a layout of both parts of the Ghetto, and that layout is entirely present to her, probably more present than
any other city or portion thereof where she lived before
or after the war.

I do not have this knowledge, and as I am listening to
her I feel distressed by what separates us: what she saw
and heard and experienced, and what I cannot. Ever.

"The Getto was extremely crowded. In every room of
every apartment of every house lived an entire family:
grandparents, parents, uncles, aunts, and children. Because
of how crowded it got, people would go outside, onto the
street, to be on their own for a while, to breathe some air,
and so the Getto streets also got insufferably crowded. If
a German was walking on the sidewalk, Jews were to step
down onto the road to let them through. If they did not
step down, they were cruelly beaten by the German.

"A typhoid fever epidemic broke out; it spread through lice. Dysentery was also spreading and becoming a full-blown epidemic."

She explains in her most matter-of-fact voice that dysentery does not spread through lice. I know that, and yet I am grateful for her neutral, informative, devoid-of-any-emotion tone. The remark is a welcome pause—respite. Her tone, her voice steady me.

"People were dying like flies in the Getto from typhoid fever. Both of Hala's aunts died. It was spreading fast and there was no recourse. They would check into a hospital and die there. And yet some survived!"

She sounds surprised, still, after all those years! I listen to her surprise; do I detect the relief of having survived? I will never experience any of this as I was born mainly to listen to this dark story over and over again, 'til it loses some of its power over her. And maybe one day over me too?

"People felt the urge to get out of their tiny, congested quarters. They would walk in the desperately crowded streets. Returning home after these 'outings,' I would take my coat off and inspect it attentively, carefully, for lice."

More Hunger—*Głód*

"EVERYONE WAS HUNGRY. DREADFULLY HUNGRY. All the time. Flora and I would try to give each other the thicker slice of bread when we were lucky to have some, and we would cry out of spite when the other refused the bigger slice.

"We would sometimes prepare some noodles (*kluski*) at home; I did not have a clue as to how to go about it, and Sonia, your grandmother who had lost a lot of weight since the beginning of the war (some thirty kilograms), your grandmother who was so ill, was laughing joyfully at my awkward efforts. Your grandmother had the gift of joy."

I wonder whether my mother, when telling her story, missed her mother exactly as I am missing mine right now as I retell it. Was it the empty-chest feeling? Was it the ache in the gut, dull and persistent?

"I remember the kitchen in the tiny apartment, and I remember my mother's beautiful hands as she was preparing the noodles, the perfectly equal flat strips, her precise measured motions, and my admiration."

I wish I could hear, even for a moment, my grandmother's sparkling laughter in the darkness of it all. I wish that this laughter of hers, this shimmering energy, could keep on illuminating the horror of the story. I miss my grandmother, whom I never met.

"Our relative, Eliasz R., came over one night for a visit and stole some of these noodles. We never said anything to him. He was very hungry. After that incident, however, whenever he visited us, we watched so that he would not steal again. He died in a most ironic way: he was to show a document to a German policeman; someone gave him a push, he lost his balance and pushed in turn the German, who killed Eliasz for this gesture of perceived disrespect.

"The hunger persisted; it was there all the time. We were selling everything we owned to buy food: tablecloths, pillowcases, clothing. We dreamt of a freshly baked loaf of rye bread, we imagined a chunk of golden butter, we obsessed about milk and eggs. We were starved; our thoughts, our fantasies, were fixated on images of meals. We were intensely hungry and painfully aware there was, and would be, very little food in the days and months to come. Whenever you looked into another's eyes, before noticing fear or despair, you saw hunger. This constant feeling of deprivation was torture.

"Once a day, we would go to a soup kitchen, and there we would get soup: lots of salty water and a couple of pieces of a rotten potato. Jews got only rotten potatoes," she adds (as if this observation is needed only because of my persistent, stubborn ignorance).

"If you happened to be particularly lucky, you would get a bone in your soup, and sometimes attached to the bone you would find a tiny bit of meat. When you got the bone, you just sucked it and chewed on it for as long as you possibly could."

When my children were little, my mother would explain to them that the meat and the cartilage near the bone were the very best parts, that they ought to try it. I think she must have continued chewing and savouring this lucky, rare, soup kitchen bone for years. None of my children seems to appreciate cartilage or bones.

"Sometimes someone would take a bit of soup from the soup kitchen for a sick relative at home, and if on the way a bit of the soup spilled, the poor would gather around to lick it off the sidewalk."

She re-enacts the licking of the soup as she recreates the scene in her mind, her tongue rolling in and out, hovering above the table on which I am taking notes, and which she pretends is, for the sake of this painful demonstration, the sidewalk.

I shudder at the memory of the re-enactment. My mother was never a convincing actress: there was something painfully mechanical, stiff, and naive in her awkwardness. Invariably I would cringe when witnessing these occasional failed performances. She loosened up toward the end of her life, and her acting, as well as acting up, became more authentic. An underappreciated bonus of her dementia.

"Some young children (as young as four or five) were sent outside the Getto walls to buy or, more often, to steal bread. By then the Getto had walls surrounding it, and not just a fence."

I panic; I realize once again that I will never get it all. In my mind the Ghetto was still surrounded by a fence! No matter how much she tells me, no matter how many times, no matter how much of it I manage to absorb, never!

"The children sent to fetch bread understand everything; they know they might get shot. The German police who guard the Getto's exits pretend sometimes not to see the children; some of them turn their heads the other way. Not always, though. Sometimes they shoot the little ones, and those small bodies are left lying there 'til the following day.

"If someone was walking down the street holding a parcel under their arm, the poor would bite into it. If indeed it was bread, then no one would take it from the poor once they had bitten into it." Why not? Was it because of fear of some transmittable illness? Or was it because of some remnant of humanity? "But if the parcel was an old shoe you had just had repaired, or some other such thing, the poor, disappointed and angry, would throw it onto the ground and you could pick it up and be on your way.

"A young boy stole an entire loaf of bread from some-where, and several others, stronger than he was and as hungry, beat him up, grabbed the loaf of bread away from him, and kept beating him up."

Her blue eyes show her astonishment at the ferocity of the boys; why, having already taken the loaf away, did the boys feel the need to beat up the original thief?

I wish I had interrupted her, discussed some of it, asked various questions, but I hardly ever dared to. Was it because I feared her impatience, or because I was afraid that the story would never end?

"In the Getto, starving people were sprawled across the sidewalk, so that passersby could not pretend not to see them. Their children were lying down beside them, also across the sidewalk."

Her voice rises to a higher pitch. Is she about to cry? How can I take on this memory so that it releases its grip on her? She is not going to cry. Her voice, desperate for a moment, is now angry. This familiar anger is better. I am relieved and reassured.

"The starving babies had tiny, very old-looking faces. They looked like minuscule old people: their eyes were deeply sunken, their faces were wrinkled. In the summer light, I could see their skull and their skeleton through their skin, but in the winter they were wrapped in rags and only their monkey-like tiny faces showed. Little animal faces. Sometimes their abdomens were distended from hunger. They were dying on the sidewalks. Occasionally a German soldier would come to the Getto simply to relish the sight of our hopeless misery. Every morning the dead were covered in newspapers. Later in the day, the streets were cleaned, the corpses were removed to make room for the new, fresh dead."

Trzynastka (Number 13)

"IN THE GETTO, AT LESZNO STREET 13, THE Germans created a special office. *Trzynastka* was a German office and it employed only Getto Jews. It was a big office, and those Jews who worked there did a meticulously thorough job. The Germans succeeded in killing most of the influential Jews in the Getto—those who had money and those who had contacts and who therefore could have tried to escape. The Jews who worked there for the Germans were scum, human scum—no principles, no integrity. Edek K. and Maks F. worked there."

I knew these two men: in normal times, they appeared to be like everyone else. There was absolutely no way to tell them apart from the rest of humanity. They were ordinary.

Perhaps a little sleazier than some, perhaps not. They were just two men—the sad banality of it all.

"Those who worked in the infamous office were to provide the Germans with the names and addresses of the most affluent Jews in the Getto, as well as with the details of their possessions. They were to denounce those who had some contacts with the Germans.

"Frequently, on a Friday night (the evening leading into the Shabbat) at suppertime, after the curfew (*godzina policyjna*), German policemen would show up at the Jewish homes designated by those who worked at the *Trzynastka* office." It occurs to me now that this could be one of the reasons my mother adamantly refused to celebrate Friday nights. "They would take the head of the household outside, about one hundred metres away from where they lived, onto the street, and everyone knew, and everyone dreaded, what was inevitably coming; they would shoot him to death (everyone was waiting in silence and terror for the sound of the shotgun). They would leave the body on the street overnight. The Germans wanted to make sure that those rich Jews, who potentially could buy their way out of the Getto and save their own lives and the lives of their families, were all dead.

"The *Trzynastka* office had the task to designate those rich Jews. Those employed by the office kept it a secret that they worked there, but people knew."

I can still see Edek's and Maks's faces in front of me. There was no shame in their eyes. While it was a secret that they had worked there, after the war those secrets became common knowledge. They would wake up in the morning and would get out of bed, look in the mirror, and everything seemed fine; lightning did not strike them, their consciences did not seem to torment them. And, once they settled in Israel, their Friday evenings, as for all other Israelis, marked the beginning of the Shabbat. They went out on Friday nights to relax, to be in the company of friends, or to play bridge.

Wife of an Officer

"HERMANN GÖRING ANNOUNCED THAT WIVES of prisoners of war detained in German Oflags (*die Offizierslager*) would not be killed. I was one of those wives. We each got a special document stating that our husband was in an Oflag." Marian, the man who would be my father, was in Oflag IIC, in Woldenberg, now Dobiegniew. "All these women, wives of the officers, were to move together into the same building in the Getto. Though a building was selected, the plan to move all the officers' wives was never realized."

Why did Göring announce that? How were those officers' wives of relevance or benefit to him? This story seems somehow incomplete. It appeared that Felek G., the Jewish lawyer, who was also in the Warsaw Ghetto and who later lived in Paris, was somehow involved. My mother had great respect for him. Celina P., one of my mother's friends, was one of the officers' wives.

Only now that all of them have died do I have questions. Only now do I give myself permission to actually think about all of this and to articulate questions about it. Before, when they were still alive, it all felt sacred and untouchable. Why? Was it the child listening who decided this? Was it the absolute authority of a very stern mother who imposed this uneasy silence? Was each question considered to be a desecration? (By me? By her?) Was a question equated with mutiny? (By her? By me?) At any rate, it seemed clear to me that my role was to listen, not to ask questions.

Does it matter now? I guess she was clinging to this document that stated that her husband was in an Oflag. Perhaps she believed it could at least buy her time.

"A Jewish policeman in the Getto also offered to marry me because wives of policemen were not deported to work camps." Who was this man? Did he know that she was married? Did she consider this marriage as a possibility? Did they have an affair? Why is she telling me this? And since she is telling me this, why is she not telling me more?

Umschlagplatz

"ALL OF THIS HAPPENED BEFORE THE *Umschlagplatz* had been established, even before Jews were ordered to give away all their jewellery, their furs, their prized possessions. They were to give all those to the Germans so they would have less 'negotiating power.' The Germans took away an incredible amount of loot to Germany. Obviously there was never a receipt given for any of these."

Why would the Germans bother to issue receipts for this loot if the original owners were all to be exterminated? On the other hand, did the Germans not document any of this for orderly and organized redistribution? Or perhaps they did and then destroyed such evidence?

"After the war, it was impossible to prove that these things had indeed been taken away and from whom."

Just material things, I think to myself, just objects;
nevertheless, I imagine an Austrian or a German woman
my age, born, like me, after the war, wearing at this very
moment my grandmother's earrings, my grandmother's
brooch, and I wonder whether this woman suspects,
whether she cares, how she got this jewellery.

"The *Umschlagplatz* was not far from a hospital and
next to a railway; freight trains were waiting, and the
Germans would push people inside the train cars with the
backs of their guns; they would hit them and push them.
The doors sealed with bars. Some of the Jews died right
there, before or immediately after getting onto the train.
The Jews were deported to death camps—Auschwitz,
Treblinka, and many others—to be gassed."

How could this otherwise apparently 'normal' woman
tell such horror stories to a child? Though, it seems to me
she could not help but tell them. What choice did she
have? What choice did I have?

"The first announcement was made on July 22, 1942: all
mentally ill people from the asylums were to be herded to
the *Umschlagplatz*."

How did she remember these dates? How did she
do that?

"Most sighed a sigh of relief; this new decree con-
cerned only those who had mental 'issues' and no one else.

"The next 'call' was for the old and the handicapped. A
woman I knew, Dorota P., an only child, had old parents.
She loved them deeply. When the elderly were ordered

to gather at the *Umschlagplatz*, Dorota's parents begged her to please help them die, in their own bed, in their own apartment. They asked her to turn on the gas in their apartment (they were afraid they would not have the courage) and then leave and shut the door behind her. They took some sleeping pills, and she did what they had asked her to do: she turned on the gas and left the apartment. Dorota survived the war and ended up in an asylum.

"Then the Germans gathered the sick. When it was the children's turn, their mothers who were unable to hide them would accompany the children to the *Umschlagplatz* to die.

"Those in the Getto who could prove that they were employed did not have to get on the train yet. Some Jews worked for the Germans outside the Getto and would leave the Getto every morning and would return at night. They were spared for now.

"People tried desperately to obtain a certificate to show that they were employed by the Germans. Those who were lucky and had such a document could still remain in the Getto."

She continues her telling in her steady, somewhat monotonous voice. She has told me all of this before. This time, however, I am taking notes. She is counting on me, reluctant as I am, to tell it one day. I feel crushed by the responsibility. I feel crushed by the story, entangled by her 'reasonable' insanity, trapped and crushed.

"There were operations (*akcje*). Apartment buildings in the Getto usually surrounded a courtyard on all four sides.

A large gate at the front would make the courtyard accessible to cars. The Germans would arrive at a courtyard in a car and yell out an order on loudspeakers for everyone to come down. Then some of the Germans would run to search apartments. Once everyone was gathered in the courtyard, they were forced to run to the *Umschlagplatz*.

"Everyone was terribly, permanently starved. When the Germans announced that anyone who would come voluntarily to the *Umschlagplatz* would get three loaves of bread, each loaf weighing a kilogram, and one kilogram of beet marmalade, people went to the *Umschlagplatz*; they wanted to eat before they died. They actually suspected it was a trap; however, they could not resist the temptation."

I wonder whether my mother had always loved bread, and especially the crusty end of a loaf, or whether she started loving it during the war? Didn't she tell me that as a child she was fussy and hardly ate anything?

"Some doors to certain rooms were hidden by wardrobes; women who had children were not allowed to hide there as the children could cry and endanger all those hiding. Therefore, more women with children than men came down to the courtyards and left with the Germans.

"The Germans made those gathered run in rows to the *Umschlagplatz*. Some women begged those who were in the hiding spaces to allow them to hide with their children, promising that they would not let their children cry; they then became responsible for all the others hiding in the room. If their baby or small child started crying in the hiding space, the mother would cover its little mouth, and the child would choke to death. I once saw a child bluish-purple because of the choking, but not dead yet.

"I would hide in these spaces; I never went down to the courtyard. The Germans would check the apartments to verify that everyone had gone down. If a baby was left behind in an apartment, the Germans simply threw the baby out the window. If a mother was there with the baby, they would first throw the baby out of the window and then kill the mother.

"We sat there in these rooms, behind the wardrobes, too scared to move, too scared to breathe. We'd hear the Germans' heavy boots coming up the stairs and into the apartment. We were shaking with fear. I can still hear the boots coming up the stairs."

This is where I stumble. She will always hear the German boots. I will just hear the story of the sound of those boots.

"It took about half an hour each time, between the first yelled-out order to come down to the courtyard 'til the sound of the German boots going back down the stairs. Someone would then come and move the *szafa* (wardrobe) so that we could open the door and get out of our hiding place."

I remember hiding as a child (in Łódź, in the third-floor apartment where we lived), in the wardrobe in my room, when my parents' maid, an alcoholic, had a delirium tremens episode and my parents called an ambulance.

I do not remember the woman's name, nor do I remember her face; her wild, animal-like screams as the paramedics were getting her into a straitjacket still resonate in my chest. The screaming was accompanied by the red, rotating ambulance lights coming from the street and illuminating rhythmically and in succession various spots in the otherwise dark room: the floor, the walls, the ceiling. I could see these lights and hear the screams through the crack of the shut doors of the wardrobe. I was perhaps five years old, and my dread, my terror, were immense. I remember her yelling as the paramedics went downstairs with her to the ambulance. I still can hear the siren's howl disappearing into the distance, further and further away. I now felt safe to get out of the wardrobe. My parents, in the chaos of it all, had not noticed I had been hiding.

A couple of years later (I was perhaps seven), it was evening and I was doing my homework, feeling especially safe. A long and frightening doorbell ringing interrupted this quiet time. While both my parents went to open the front door, I disappeared once again into my hiding place. Its tight darkness felt comforting. I heard the voice of our upstairs neighbours' son, Andrzej, a ten-year-old boy; he was sobbing and sounded distressed. My father left with Andrzej and our apartment was quiet again for a short while. Then the howling ambulance arrived, paramedics were running fast up the stairs and a while later went down the stairs slowly. Again the siren, and the ambulance left.

My father came back from the neighbours', and I heard him telling my mother that Andrzej's father had collapsed and died; he said that the paramedics could not do anything, no one could; it was over.

This tiny, dark wardrobe in my room where I discovered madness, violence, and death, was a type of hiding place replicating in a strange manner the madness and death my mother had experienced several years earlier while hiding, terrorized, in that space behind the wardrobe in the Ghetto. I can still recreate that wardrobe in my mind. And the terror. *Zgroza*.

"The Getto was shrinking all the time as people were dying or getting killed and others were being deported to work camps, concentration camps, and extermination camps. Certain areas of the Getto were no longer necessary, and the Germans would 'close' those areas; they would cease to be part of the Getto.

"By 1942, the Getto was completely shut off, sealed tight; no one could come in or get out. As I already mentioned, the Germans had started sending Jews from the *Umschlagplatz* to camps. I think that on July 22, 1942, posters appeared; the Germans would be taking people to work camps.

"The day following this announcement Adam Czerniakow committed suicide by swallowing cyanide. He was sixty-two years old. Czerniakow was the Chair of the Jewish Council in the Getto. He understood what the announcement signified. He refused to cooperate with the

Germans. News in the Getto travelled very fast. Everyone knew about Czerniakow's death; they knew it meant that the end was near."

How is it conceivable that a few years after this last retelling of the story my mother's extraordinarily sharp mind was irrevocably broken: she was demented.

The Escape

"AT THE SOUP KITCHEN ON LESZNO STREET, we met my mother's relative, the poet Itzhak K. He said that the end was close and that all three of us needed to escape from the Getto. I arranged for my mother and my sister to escape. I stayed behind to pack a few of our belongings and to send the packages to them."

I could have asked how they escaped. I could have asked what belongings she packed, and how she sent them, and to what address. I did not.

"There were a few crossings to and from the Getto, guarded by the Ukrainian or Lithuanian black-clad soldiers or by the German police. Around five in the morning, groups of workers left the Getto for factories in

Warszawa. There were typically about thirty people in this
kind of a group.

"I paid a Jewish man who was leading such a group of
workers. I paid him 500 *złotych*. Eliasz gave me the money.
He had married a rich woman in the Getto in the hope
that this would help him survive. It did not.

"It was August 26, 1942. I put a scarf on my head and
carried an almost-empty backpack in order to look like a
factory worker. The workers left the Getto in the morning
and returned at night, so the backpack had to be empty
to avoid suspicion. I was shaking: if the guards stopped
me, they would shoot me on the spot. I don't believe that
I looked remotely like a factory worker (*robotnica*). When
I got to the factory, I went to see the supervisor. I told her
that I had gone to visit someone in the Getto and that
I returned with the workers that morning. She did not
appear to suspect me, was amazed by my courage to visit
someone in the Getto, and let me go."

What factory was it? How could I not have asked? She
was right to be distressed about my listening.

"I had two contacts, the first one was a phone number
of Hanka Klein, my cousin. The second was an address of a
Polish man, Pan Zygmunt Kostro (a practising Catholic),
who was the Getto's *komornik* (bailiff, responsible for rents
and taxes for the Getto).

"I first called Hanka, but she said she could not let me
sleep at her place. She gave me Ania's number (Hanka's husband's sister); she said that I could go to Ania's place, as her

landlady was not home, and that I was to hide in Ania's room and not make any noise. I then went to see Pan Kostro, my second contact; I had memorized his address (nothing was to be written down in case one got caught).

"I arrived at Kostro's address; it was a lawyer's office. I was sitting in the waiting room, as Kostro had a client in his office with him. The door to the office was half open. Through it he was watching me attentively while attending to his client.

"When I got into his office, I begged him to help my friend Eliza R. to leave the Getto. I knew that he had seen Eliza a few months earlier in the Getto (she was a family friend of his). But at the time, Eliza could not leave her sick sister, Aniela, on her own. Aniela had tuberculosis and fever when Pan Kostro visited Eliza in the Getto. Meanwhile, the Germans had deported the sister, Aniela, to a concentration camp and must have gassed her as she was Jewish, had TB, and was a hunchback as well. Each one of the conditions was reason enough for the Germans to kill her. A hunchback, obviously…"

Her unfinished sentence constitutes an acknowledgement of my limited understanding. It crosses my mind that Piotr, my dead brother, could have perhaps listened and understood better. I feel exasperated; her expectations of me, and her disappointment, seem immense. And, as is often the case, she appears to be devastatingly right.

"So I concluded: Eliza is begging for help; she wants to live. Pan Kostro responded that I must be mistaken, that

he did not know Eliza R., nor any other person by this
name; he said he had no idea what I was talking about.
And then, '*A kim właściwie Pani jest?*' ('And who, actually,
are you, Madam?') Who *are you???*

"I could not count on his help without revealing the
truth about me to him. So I told him I was Jewish, had
no papers, no name on the Aryan side. He believed me.
Pan Kostro promised that he would try to help Eliza.
From that day on, he would go twice a day to the Getto;
I would come twice a day to see him and to find out
whether he had succeeded.

"The guards would not let him into the Getto, as
Christians were no longer permitted entry. And so, Eliza,
the quiet, unassuming, lovely woman, was deported, like
her sister, to a concentration camp—deported and gassed.
In the meanwhile, Hanka, my cousin, bought for me,
from a church, a birth certificate and an ID of a deceased
woman, Aleksandra Karpińska."

Oh my God, why did I think that Zygmunt Kostro
had provided my mother with a false ID? Has there been
another version of the story? Was I now getting the final,
'official' version? Was it, once again, my listening that was
flawed, faulty? At this point in time I can only assume
responsibility for any such discrepancies. So my mother
owed her life to, among others, Hanka? She never actually
directly acknowledged that; was it Hanka and her mer-
cantile, petty disposition? Was it a more generalized reluctance to acknowledge that she owed her life, even in part,

to a Jewish woman, her relative? Her deep dislike of Jews, her self-hatred, came as an additional 'fringe benefit' of the story and have accompanied me all my life.

"A few days after I met Zygmunt Kostro for the very first time, he introduced me to his wife, Janina, and daughter, Teresa. The family befriended me. I could come to see them with any concerns I had. They were warm and caring, they offered support, and they helped whenever and however they could. Zygmunt assured me that, if ever I was caught by the Gestapo, he would go to the Gestapo in person and testify that he knew my family and that I was a pure Aryan and a Christian. He had a whole story ready for me. This willingness to provide verification of my false identity could have cost the entire Kostro family their lives."

I wish I could hear this story. I wish I could now ask her for it. This story, like so many others, has fallen into the ever-triumphant domain of the silence of death. Now, as I approach my own death, I think I could finally be ready to hear it. Zygmunt and Janina Kostro are listed at Yad Vashem as Righteous Among the Nations. My mother sent her testimony to honour them.

"Zygmunt arranged for a family to rent a room to me and to Flora. He lied and assured his friends that we were Christians. It helped us tremendously: for Christians, renting a room was not expensive; however, for Jews the rent, and the risk, was excessively high. And so very few were willing to take the risk and, when they did, the price was exorbitant."

The Good Look

/

"*DOBRY WYGLĄD*—'THE GOOD LOOK.' I LOOKED 'right'; I had the 'good Aryan look'; I did not look Jewish."

Indeed, I can see her face: blond hair, light-blue eyes, fair skin, regular features, small, straight nose. I recall getting into a taxi with her, in Zurich, at the airport. She was already in her eighties; we were on our way to Canada. The driver asked us where we had come from. She told him we were coming back from Tel Aviv and that we had been visiting relatives.

The taxi driver expressed his complete astonishment, looked at her in the rear-view mirror, and he said, "You, Jewish? It cannot be." Then, turning to look at me in the rear-view mirror, said, "Her, I could guess, but you, never!"

I remember her deep satisfaction: she still had the 'good Aryan look'! There was something in that satisfaction which felt like smugness. There was a moral righteousness and, yes, some gloating in how she felt about her appearance: looking Gentile seemed to give her moral superiority over others less fortunate (or less deserving?), including myself.

"'Good looks' were looks which did not betray one's Semitic origins. Poles were often blond and blue-eyed; I had a small nose—it was not long, and it was not humped. I moved like a non-Jew.

"Jews were built differently. Jewish women moved differently."

How do Jews move? What on earth is she talking about? If it were not my mother talking, would I even be listening to this?

I dare ask, "How? How did they move? What was different about their movements?" She gets agitated. I am challenging her, questioning the truth of her statement. Neither one of us is used to this.

"The Jewish beggars in the Getto always harassed my sister, Flora, never me!"

Is this proof? Of what? She senses my reluctance to agree; I feel her impatience and her resignation: I am her only dedicated listener, the last one.

She will not tell her story this way to anyone else; it is her gift to me once again. It is her story, after all, and for the very last time she has control over it. She trusts me with her gift, and I am deeply touched by her trust. In spite of my questions and my doubts. In spite of challenging her. There is something profoundly, terribly poignant and sad about her confiding in me, choosing me above all others, me and my imperfect listening.

"Jewish faces are more mobile in their expressions, more engaged. I used to explain to your Aunt Flora, 'Look at me, have an expressionless look, have a vacant look, do not think about anything.'"

My mother had a naturally 'blank' face. I frequently felt I needed to check: "Have you heard what I just said?" "Were you listening?" "What do you think about what I just told you?" Her eyes remained calm, unperturbed, and so blue. Her face remained still. I remember walking beside her, first in Poland, then in Israel, then in the rest of Europe and in Canada, and she would point at people and remark, "Look, a Jew." "Look, with a face like hers she would not have survived the war." "With such a body, with those gestures, he would have been sent to a concentration camp." Over and over again, this obsessive, compulsive screening, this constant racial differentiation which she did not control. Her concern that my hair not be frizzy— yet another Jewish characteristic.

I once dared ask her, "Do you think I could have survived?"

"Maybe hidden in a convent, but not on the Aryan side (*nie po aryjskiej stronie*)," she responded.

Did I detect a hint of condescension, or did I just

imagine that? She did, after all, send me to a French convent school in Jaffa a few years after our arrival to Israel.

"Your eyes are not blue enough, your features are not regular enough," she said, and she sounded so categorical.

She was happy with her appearance: it helped her survive. She was not identified as a Jew thanks to her 'good look.' She seemed to view the 'good look' as a moral quality, as a virtue. It had helped her during the war. Her strange pride in this Aryan look stayed with her throughout her entire life.

I can still hear the satisfaction and pride in her voice, as if it were not mere luck. It was not simply about beauty; occasionally she would acknowledge that there were indeed some very attractive Jews with a Semitic appearance. I suppose that, to her, having a Jewish look was similar to wearing a yellow Star of David patch.

Stories from the Aryan Side

"FOR A SHORT WHILE I LIVED WITH HANKA AND her sister-in-law, Lusia, who was Mietek's wife. Mietek lived on his own in a tiny apartment. No one went to see him but me. He would read his Hebrew poems to me, and I would tell him that I did not understand; he would ask me to listen to the rhythm."

There is something infinitely sad about all of this, about her, of all people, in her down-to-earth pragmatism, listening to Mietek's poems, written and read in Hebrew. Mietek was killed, and the poems got lost. I wonder what kind of poems these were; I suspect they were lyrical, in which case it was better, more merciful, that they were in Hebrew, as my mother seemed to have a low tolerance for lyrical musings and she would have made sure to deflate any soaring romantic expressions had they been in Polish.

"Hanka was a mediocre actress. She had married a chemical engineer, who at the beginning of the war escaped Poland and left a chemical factory to Hanka. She was still getting an income from this factory. She also owned three apartments. She needed me to help her collect the money from the factory and to help her hide her entire family. I could help, as my Polish was impeccable and because I looked like a Pole."

I sense that my mother dislikes Hanka profoundly. I sense her condemnation, yet this woman was instrumental in saving my mother's life. My mother quotes her mother Sonia to discredit Hanka. My grandmother felt that Hanka was a better actress in life than on stage. There is an animosity, an aversion. I will probably never understand the true source of these feelings. I don't even know which pieces are missing to complete the picture.

"In one of her three apartments Hanka was hiding her mother, Mirka L. Mirka had false papers and was hiding on the Aryan side."

She laughs: not the bitter laughter, not the cynical one, just laughter, light and sparkly and rare. This is a moment I miss.

"I was to live with Hanka's mother, Aunt Mirka, to do her errands and represent her when dealing with the superintendents. Aunt Mirka's name (on the false papers) was Antonina. She was Pani Antonina (Mrs. Antonina) to the world.

"Twice a week Pani Antonina would send me to buy a Russian newspaper for her. Very often it was disappointing—the newspaper would be sold out. Aunt Mirka had already been hiding for a few months as 'Pani Antonina' when, upon returning from my unsuccessful 'mission' to buy her the Russian newspaper, I said to her, 'Poor Pani Antonina, she never gets to read her newspaper!' She looked at me, puzzled, confused, and astonished. 'Who, on earth, is Pani Antonina?!' I felt like laughing and crying at the same time. She just could not remember her false name, even though her life depended on it.

"A while later Aunt Mirka's other daughter, Niusia P., and her husband, Jerzy, moved in with Aunt Mirka and me. They had returned to Warszawa from the east, where they had been working. One evening we heard the all-too-familiar and terrorizing sound of heavy German boot steps. Then a scream and a horrible noise; a person from a floor above us had jumped out the window to her death. She did not want to be caught by the Germans.

"Then the heavy boot steps came down the stairs, to our floor. The German police were knocking on the door of our apartment. I went to the door and opened it. I asked the Germans standing at the door what the problem was, and they explained that some light was coming through one of our windows. We were to correct it, as the blackout was to be complete, they said. I promised them that I would rectify the situation immediately and, luckily, they did not ask to inspect the apartment!

"With significant relief I went back in, and what I saw appeared to me both absurd and hilarious. Niusia was hiding under the covers in one bed while Aunt Mirka and her son-in-law, Jerzy, were in the other bed together, their heads sticking out from under the covers; Jerzy's moustache constituted the focal point. I still remember how comical the moustache looked."

I admire my mother's cool courage, her seeming fearlessness, her ability to appear calm and collected when circumstances were horrific. Her strength inspires me even now. What I miss, though, even more than her bravery, is her rare laughter; it was mostly dark. Yet wasn't it a true miracle that she laughed at all? Her laughter was such an infrequent guest in our home during the years I was growing up. I craved it; its black light surprisingly managed to illuminate some inky corners; was it the suspension in her anger?

"In Warszawa I met Jurek K.; he was friendly and charming. He warned me that the town where Sonia and Flora were hiding, Wierzbnik Starachowice, was also becoming very dangerous for Jews. They were going to establish a getto there. He felt that I ought to bring them both to Warszawa.

"I went to Hanka and asked her to help me. She stated categorically that she would not allow either my mother or my sister in any of her apartments. She appeared irritated that I would dare to want to save my mother and my sister."

Such ugly behaviour would explain my mother's condemnation of Hanka. I feel, paradoxically, a measure of relief.

"I asked Hanka to provide me with false ID papers for both my mother and my sister. Flora was terrified to travel to Warszawa. My mother said she would come if I accompanied them. We took the train. On the way, my mother had a heart attack. She later told me that she was afraid she would die on the way, on the train, and that I would have to bury her without any ID."

This story, these two extraordinarily courageous women, my grandmother and my mother, on the train.

"In Warszawa, my mother and I had a place to stay for a couple of days. So we went out to look for an apartment. On our way, however, we were followed by blackmailers and had to give them all the money we had on us.

"I had no choice. I went back to Hanka; we desperately needed a place. She found us a room at the superintendent's. The woman had just had a baby. Sonia helped care for the baby, so the woman was quite happy. But we had to keep on moving; we were on the run. My mother wrote down the Lord's Prayer. *Ojcze Nasz...* (Our Father who art in heaven...). This was to serve as proof that she was Christian. The following day she had it perfectly memorized, and she commented on how beautiful this prayer was."

I wish I could have met my grandmother. Somehow, who I am seems intertwined with who she was. My mother tried to describe her several times, but the descriptions left out the details I needed to successfully bring her to life.

"In Milanówek, a hiding spot got freed up. Zygmunt told us about it. It was a large house with lots of small units. The landlords, the Bogdańskis, said that they would let Sonia, my mother, stay there, on one condition: that no Jew was ever to visit her. My mother said that she had only one daughter, Flora. She explained to the landlords that I was just a Christian friend.

"And so, when she was dying there, she told the land-lords, 'Ola (diminutive of Aleksandra, my false name) will not despair; she is not my daughter, but my daughter, Flora, will be inconsolable.' Sonia remained lucid 'til her last breath."

My mother was proud of her mother, of her lucidity, in the same way I used to be proud of my mother's lucidity. I now wish I could ask more questions about my grand-mother Sonia. What voice did she have—and was it any-thing like my mother's and my own? What kinds of songs did she like to sing? What kinds of books did she like to read? What made her laugh? What made her cry? Is it possible to miss her even though I never met her? She made sure 'til her last breath not to endanger my mother's life by revealing she was Jewish.

My mother concludes this story with a non sequitur: "The landlord, Bogdański, a Catholic, a Christian, was

killed by the Germans; they claimed he was a communist."
How did my mother find out about it? When? Is that why
the landlord agreed to hide my grandmother, because he
was a Christian? Because he was a communist? Or was it
for the money? Or did he do it for all those reasons?

"So my mother, Sonia, was at the Bogdańskis', where
she was hiding. She was very cold, she was hungry, and her
heart was hurting terribly. I arranged for a doctor to visit
her to see whether he could help; he told me that Sonia's
heart was failing and that she was dying.

"The day she died, I was told that she got out of bed
and told Pani Bogdańska to phone me, Ola, and say that
this was the end. The message was to her non-Jewish
friend: 'I am dying, please save my daughter, Flora.' I had
told my mother that I would go with Flora to Germany.
My mother understood that I was not going to Germany
because of her. Her message to me via Pani Bogdańska
was unequivocal: 'As soon as I die, please do everything
you can to save her.'

"My mother died on November 23, 1942. She was buried
in Milanówek under her false name, Franciozka Wolańska.
After the war her real name, Zofia Knopf, was also
engraved on the tombstone."

What courage in the face of death. My grandmother
and my mother. My heroines.

The day I will visit my grandmother's grave in
Milanówek is coming. A day for which I have waited for a
long time. A day for which I have prepared. A necessary day.

Interestingly, it is Róża and Piotr, Zygmunt's granddaughter and grandson, who are looking after my grandmother's grave in Milanówek.

I will then go to Tel Aviv to the cemetery where Flora is buried. I will tell her about my visit to her mother's grave. I will tell her how it went. Finally, I will travel to Ontario where I buried my mother's ashes. Just to reassure her, to tell her I visited the two other graves.

Scattered. So far apart. So close. All three in my heart. The graves are not abandoned. I will put a few little stones on each. To honour each one of them.

More Hunger—*Głód*

"WE WERE WALKING WITH LUSIA IN WARSZAWA, chatting and telling each other how hungry we were."

My mother interrupts this story to make a comment: "Lusia had a Jewish accent when she spoke Polish; I kept telling her to slow down and enunciate each sound as clearly as she could."

Grimacing, my mother imitates a Jewish accent in Polish. She is profoundly hurt by this recollection, as well as by her own intransigent, cruel judgment. With each breath she draws she prolongs our suffering. I listen, helpless, to this tragic and humiliating imitation.

"So Lusia and I were describing to each other how hungry we were and the kinds of food we craved. Lusia was dreaming of something sweet; I coveted some butter.

"When we finally reached Hanka's apartment, we saw a large loaf of bread on the table and next to it some lard. Hanka allowed us to take a slice of bread each. (Bread was precious; however, lard [*smalec*] was even more so, and provided valuable nourishment—although bread would make you full faster.) As we were devouring our bread, Hanka commented on how humble and modest Lusia was: 'She took a thicker slice of bread than Ola did, so as not to take extra lard!' Lusia was so upset that she stopped eating altogether. I had trouble swallowing, but kept on chewing: I could not afford to stop; I had to eat."

False Names,
Hiding, and Death

"JĘDREK, NIUSIA'S FIVE-YEAR-OLD SON (NIUSIA was Hanka's sister), was to be brought to the railway station. He was to take the train to a Christian family in a small town called Prószków (on the Warszawa–Otwock line). They promised to hide the little blond Jewish boy in exchange for payments."

She can see the child as she tells me the story. I wish I could too. No matter how much she describes him, I will never see him. I feel defeated.

"Trustingly, he gave me his little hand. I asked him, 'Jędrusiu, do you know who I am?' He nodded silently. 'Do you know my name?' I asked. 'Yes,' he whispered. 'Can you tell me?'" She wanted to hear her real name spoken; she craved hearing her real name spoken by a child. She needed to feel recognized.

"He said he would whisper the name in my ear. And he did. 'Stefa. You were Stefa before, but I don't know your name now.'" It must have been a relief to hear her name, to know that, despite the terror, the child recognized her.

"Before going onto the train, Jędrek turned to me and said, 'If you see my *mamusia*, tell her that I love her very much.' We both were crying.

"Even in our dreams, when we were on the Aryan side my sister Flora and I called each other by our false ID names. Ola was my name; Flora's was Wala.

"When two Jewish people met on the street, even if they were very good friends, they would never reveal to each other their new Aryan false name. This was so that, if caught by the Gestapo, they would not be able to reveal it. The Germans tortured Jews 'til they got the information they sought—they would beat the Jews with a whip or a club, break bones, toes, fingers, pull fingernails, stick slivers under nails, insert sticks into the rectum...."

I am no longer listening; I just cannot bear it. She is correct, though, she always had been; this is truly indisputable: if she can tell this, what right have I got to refuse to listen? She concludes as I weave my way back to listening.

"And so the victim would tell everything she or he knew, and that did not save them either. So the less one knew, the better it was. Though some did not reveal a thing. All this was not about being afraid to die, because death was much easier than the torture which preceded it.

"In 1943, the Allied forces bombed many of the military targets around Warszawa. During the first days of the war, in Łódź, I was so terrified of the air raid announcements over the radio; later on it stopped worrying me.

"When these bombings occurred, most people ran to hide in the basements of houses. Flora and I remained in our room. It was not death through a bomb which terrified us; this death was, by far, better than the death of a Jew. This death was also far better than life in constant fear that someone might discover our secret: we were Jewish. A Jew, once caught, was certain to face torture before death."

As I am listening, it occurs to me that this is a somewhat new angle on the reasons to refuse to go down to a shelter during bombings; it has to do with weighing the pros and cons of two kinds of death. It reminds me of the theory I have heard before: preferring a faster death above ground to the horrible live burial in the shelter. But here, an extra incentive to staying above ground is the potential relief through death from the cruelties and suffering inflicted by the Nazis if they suspected you were Jewish. I wonder whether all children of Holocaust survivors lived their entire lives, like I did, immersed in this type of morbid 'economics.'

The Little Boy

"LUSIA'S SISTER WANTED TO SAVE HER TWO children, a six-year-old boy and a seven-year-old girl. Both children were in Starachowice, a town which was becoming increasingly dangerous. The girl was not much of a problem, but the boy was extremely vulnerable."

I interrupt her: Was it about the 'look'? Was the boy afflicted with the Jewish 'look'? She turns to me, trying to contain her impatience and her irritation, as if I present some kind of a deficiency. My listening deficiency having been established a long time ago, her tone implies a particular disappointment, and she explains, somewhat exasperately, "Girls were not circumcised."

"The little boy spoke mostly Yiddish. He spoke hardly any Polish, and the Polish he did speak would betray him: he had a Jewish accent!"

My mother uses a highly charged anti-Semitic expression: *on żydłaczył*—snarky, deprecating, hurtful. And of course the little boy was circumcised.

My mother always held a scorn—worse, an aversion—for Yiddish, perhaps because, like the 'Jewish look,' it revealed Jews' identities and endangered their lives. The anatomy of self-hatred, the anatomy of its transmission.

"No one wanted to travel with the child from Starachowice to Warszawa. It was extremely risky, so Hanka called me. I told Hanka that I would bring the child from Starachowice to Warszawa if she would get false ID papers for Flora, as well as a place for her to stay. Hanka agreed, and so I went to Starachowice and got both Flora and the little boy back to Warszawa.

"On the train the child burst out crying. Such a beautiful tiny boy; he had the most incredible black, huge Jewish eyes. I took him to the washroom, sat him down on the toilet, gave him a candy; I told him that crying was not allowed, and he listened. I told him to look me in the eyes each time he felt scared, each time he felt like crying. For the rest of the train ride the child stayed quiet."

My mother's eyes. My mother's blue eyes. Fearless. I miss those eyes. I miss her steady gaze. I miss looking her in the eyes and absorbing her strength and courage.

"When we arrived at the railway station in Warszawa, the child's uncle picked him up to take him to a young Ukrainian couple for hiding. I visited the child daily. Very quickly he had all the Christian prayers memorized. His Polish language was improving."

Clearly my mother felt attached to the little boy. This is when I anticipate the terrible ending that I have heard before and where, with each retelling, my mother's voice breaks.

"Hanka sent the child"—What was his name?! Did she tell me? Did I sin and forget?—"to the Hotel Polski for those who wished to go to the United States. He was exterminated along with all the others who dared to dream of an escape. Who dared to trust the enemy. Who fell into the trap."

Kenkarta

"EACH PERSON IN WARSZAWA WAS REQUIRED TO have a *kenkarta* (an ID card). This was vital: we were expected to produce it each time when confronted by officials. When applying for it, one did not have to go in person to the police precinct, however, to actually obtain the card, one had to go in person.

"I helped many other Jewish people outside the Getto to apply for their *kenkarta* and, when the time came, I went with them to the police station to get it. I went with Marta L., a lawyer and a good friend of Celina P., who had helped Celina get out of the Getto. Marta asked me to accompany Celina to get her *kenkarta*, as Celina was too scared to go on her own.

"So I went to pick her up. Celina, whom I knew from before the war and from the Getto, was unrecognizable; she seemed heavier, perhaps swollen from hunger, and had incredibly skinny legs. She was wearing very dark sunglasses. I told her to take them off, as they were attracting attention, but she refused. She had—she told me—witnessed through these eyes such unspeakable horrors that they would forever be reflected in her eyes."

My mother, in her typically sharp manner, her familiar and painfully deflating way, adds, "Celina just had Jewish eyes, that's all…." I remember distinctly Celina's eyes; they were large, moist, and beautiful. The eyes were dark brown and were framed by extraordinarily long black eyelashes. My mother concludes in her down-to-earth, business-like fashion, "Celina took her sunglasses off, we got her *kenkarta*, and I escorted her home."

My mother was fearless.

Blackmailed (*Szantażowana*)

"FLORA AND I WERE WALKING ALONG ALEJE Jerozolimskie (across from the railway station). I was to take her to Pani Schumann (a *Volksdeutsche*). Pani Schumann had two little children, and Flora was going to be their nanny. Suddenly I realized we were being followed. I recognized Tadek H., the son of Hanka's maid, from a distance. He was the denunciator. Having initially, along with his mother, helped Hanka, he was now blackmailing her. He realized blackmailing was far more lucrative than simply helping.

"We were brought to the police station. Our false papers were in order. While waiting at the police station, I observed an old Jewish woman waiting there as well.

She said she just had to know whether Jehovah would win at the end."

My mother's voice reveals her bewilderment; to my mother, at that moment especially, the woman's preoccupation appeared particularly absurd. Her way of thinking seemed bizarre and incomprehensible. Fifty years later, while retelling this incident, my mother still looks perplexed and astonished. My mother's logic and this Jewish woman's faith: irreconcilable.

"The two blackmailers, Tadek H. and his friend, wanted money. I went to Hanka to ask her for help. Ania (Hanka's and Niusia's sister-in-law) brought the money. The blackmailing stopped for a brief while. Then it started again.

"Both Tadek H. and his mother, Anna H. (Hanka's maid), knew every single Jew that Hanka had helped or was helping. They had all their current addresses. In May of 1943 Tadek H. disclosed all these addresses to blackmailers."

Did he do it for a large sum of money? Did he first try to extort even more money from Hanka?

"That very day two Polish policemen and a civilian came to our door; they said that they would take us to the Gestapo. My sister Flora and I offered them a wristwatch and 1,000 *złotych*.

"Just at that moment, a friend of Flora's arrived to see her. She left and returned with the money. The name of the friend was Jaga N. (she later became a nun). Jaga N. would come to pick up Flora to walk her to work."

The terror of walking the streets. Like hunted-down animals. How do I even attempt to imagine this terror—a gut-wrenching, visceral fear? Am I capable of recreating it? Why do I feel that I owe it to myself, that I owe it to my mother and to my aunt, to recreate it, to somehow relive it?

"When the blackmailers got the watch and the money, they left, but it was quite obvious that we had to move; our money bought us merely a day. In spite of our false IDs, we were no longer able to sign in, to register as bona fide citizens.

"I went to an office at Nowy Świat 68; they were recruiting workers for Germany. The office director was Robert Strikman. Was he a *Volksdeutsche*? Was he a Jew? There was a line-up to see him. When I got to him, he asked me, 'Do you want to go to Germany?' and I answered, 'Yes, I do.' He showed me a chair on the side and told me to please sit over there. I sat down and waited. Alone. Scared. He had told no one but me to wait there.

"Then he called me back and asked why I wished to go. I made up a story. He said that they were now sending all applicants only to Kassel and that Kassel was being bombarded by the Allies. He concluded, 'I will not sign a death sentence for you,' and then added that in the line-up there was a tall, blond Jewish woman, and that she was going to become 'soap,' but that there was a young, blond Jewish man who was going to Vienna. He volunteered to ask the young Jewish man to find work for me in Vienna; he told me to return a few days later. I did.

"Nothing came of the Vienna work possibility; however, he offered to send me to work in Skierniewice. I was worried about Flora; I could not leave her behind.

"In the meantime, a Jewish woman named Jasia Słonimska, whom I went to see, promised to help me, as she had contacts with Germans, such as Anton Graf, who were helping to save Jews. She was later killed by Poles for having had contacts with Germans. In fact, and ironically, the contacts she had were with Germans who wanted to save Jews."

I can still hear her saying this, in a tone of tying up loose ends, for the sake of introducing some order in her story.

Poniewierka
(Wandering/Vagrancy)

"IT TOOK FOUR AND A HALF MONTHS FROM THE time of the beginning of being blackmailed 'til the moment I left Warszawa. During these months, I was on the run. I never knew where I would stay next, where I would sleep next, or where I would spend the following night. During these four and a half months I slept in fifty-six different places."

Did my mother remember each of the places and then count them, or did she simply keep track of each time she moved?

"During the day I tried to earn some money. I would try to peddle stockings and shoelaces. For four and a half months I just wandered (*poniewierałam się*). For a few days

I worked as a nanny for a widower who had a six-year-old girl. His wife had been killed. He was a Jew hiding as a Christian. I had a mattress on the floor; he came at night and wanted to sleep with me. I refused, and he told me to leave."

I wonder how many times my mother rejected such advances. She was a beautiful young woman. How many times she consented. What did she not tell me? And why did I feel that she owed me the whole truth? Was it implicit that I had to believe it all? Even though I was her 'designated' listener, this role she chose for me did not cancel the fact that she was my mother, that I was her daughter. Were the two roles compatible? Truly compatible?

"Then I found similar work on the Warszawa–Otwock line; I took care of two children. But the mother did not want to keep me; she felt that I was too attractive. The couple gave me a key to their Warszawa apartment and allowed me to stay there."

This is too sketchy. Something is missing, the story is not complete; maybe after all these years my mother does not remember? Though her memory is formidable. Crushingly. But maybe she really does not remember? I could certainly understand that. It would perhaps make her more vulnerable? I feel uneasy and unsettled.

"After three days in that apartment, I gave the key back to them; I was terrified of more blackmail. I went to see the *dozorca* (superintendent) a few houses away; I begged him to let me sleep there. He agreed. He was a decent man; when at night blackmailers would come to get me, he would warn me to run upstairs while he would get rid of them.

"I was often on the Warszawa–Otwock train. Gestapo people in civilian clothes (*Volksdeutsche*) came onto the train and were checking documents. (The previous day Poles had killed a German policeman.) I did not have the papers the man was asking for; I did not have an *arbeits karte*. He told me to join the group of suspect, 'paperless' people.

"I cried out, '*Proszę Pana!*' ('Please, sir!') He looked at me and told me to sit down. I was saved."

So all those chains of events, all those nameless and faceless men and women—some ruthless, some cowards, some brave and some spineless—all contributed to her survival and, therefore, to my existence.

A.K. (*Armia Krajowa*) and A.L. (*Armia Ludowa*)

"THE UNDERGROUND NEVER STOPPED ORGANIZ-
ing operations (*akcje*). An acquaintance, a Jew, gave
me a key to his apartment in Żoliborz, a neigh-
bourhood, where I would be able to stay for a few days.

"I was on my way to the apartment. When the tramway was about to arrive at the stop, the conductor brought
the tramway to a halt and told all passengers to run in the
opposite direction to that of the tram; there was a shooting and two gendarmes had been killed.

"I ran in the opposite direction, as instructed, and
stopped near the centre, Królewska i Marszałkowska, and
had no idea what to do next; the police hour (curfew) was
fast approaching.

"A Bata shoe store was right there; I had left my shoes there in the past to be repaired. The man in charge had always done a good job—reasonably and quickly. I stood there wishing I could spend the night at the Bata store. Suddenly the shoemaker from Bata appeared; I told him about the shootings and said that the only way for me to get through the night would be to sleep in the store. He said that he would let me and, even though it was not his shift, he would stay with me.

"The superintendent did not want to let me in, but he relented. The shoemaker went out and came back with bread, ham, and vodka. I ate; he drank. After drinking quite a bit, he wanted to 'make love'; I told him to go to sleep and that we would have our 'date' later. He was so drunk that I managed to convince him. I knew I had to sleep or the following day I would not 'look' good."

She recognized and acknowledged how instrumental to her survival her looks really were.

"As soon as it got light outside, I started getting ready to leave. Suddenly there was knocking on the door: two Polish-speaking secret policemen walked in. They said they were in charge of 'social behaviour'; they thought I was a prostitute. The shoemaker explained that I needed a room to sleep through the night; he promised the secret policemen to get new soles for their shoes."

As I am listening to my mother's story, I have doubts about my capability to do her justice; my listening is flawed, my memory seems unreliable, and being her daughter adds, I think, to the distortion. I am touched and humbled by her trust. Will I prove to be worthy of it?

"I left Bata and stepped into a church and thanked fate for still being alive. A few days later I went to Bata to have my shoes repaired. I inquired whether the shoemaker had made the soles for the secret policemen and I offered to reimburse him for this. The man declined; he was embarrassed to have made a fool of himself. He said Bata had paid."

This painful duet: her voice and mine, in Polish and in English, across continents and decades. Words and memories that cannot be suppressed, cannot be silenced, and I am slowly reconciling myself with her story, her biggest treasure with which she entrusts me. I am honoured. I am listening as well as I can. I am listening as if my life depends on it. It does.

"I had no place to sleep. I never knew in the morning where I would end up sleeping at night. I was not registered (*meldowana*) anymore. That is when I went to see Pani Słonimska; she promised that she would help both Flora and me to get to Germany. She told me to go see Transport Führer Anton Graf."

She says this will become a book. That is what she wants.

May 1943

"I USED TO WALK FLORA TO THE TRAMWAY STA-
tion. She was scared to walk on her own. That day in
May '43 a blackmailer was following us. He told Flora
that someone was blackmailing me as well. He took her
to the police station (a Polish police station). It was past
8:00 p.m., past *godzina policyjna* ('police hour' or curfew).
I thought I would never see Flora again and would never
know how she died...."

"She came back!" My mother's voice expresses surprise
and delight, still, some sixty years later! "She was very pale,
frightened, and shaken, but alive! She told me that an officer spoke with her. He happened to be a specialist in reli-
gions, he told her. The officer took away her *kenkarta* and
told her that if she would return to the police station the

following day and could answer all his questions about
religion (I think he meant Catholicism), he would give
the *kenkarta* back to her.

"We studied all night, and in the morning we went to
see Janina K. She said goodbye and made the sign of the
cross on Flora. Flora and I went back to the police station.
I waited for her. I was terrified that she would not come
back. The Polish officer did not ask her a single question!
He just gave the *kenkarta* back to her and wished her good
luck! We returned to our friends, Janina, Zygmunt, and
Teresa Kostro, to reassure them; we were still alive!

"My documents were no longer of any use because of
the blackmail (instigated by Tadek H.); I was on the run.
I found a tiny room for Flora in the house of an elderly
lady, on Puławska Street. There were other young Jewish
women living there. Sometimes they would leave in the
morning and never come back. We knew they had been
tortured and killed."

The Maid

"I ENTERED THE OFFICE OF ANTON GRAF. HE looked up at me and I knew that he knew that I was Jewish. There was no going back. He asked where I would like to go. I told him. He said, 'If I were *you*, I would not go there.' So I said, 'If you were *me*, where would you go?'

"He looked me in the eyes and asked whether I would be willing to be a maid. Without a moment's hesitation, I replied, 'Yes!'"

Anton Graf saved my mother's life! By doing that he was risking his life and that of his family! I wish I could meet this family; I wish I could thank them.

"Jasia Słonimska went with me to the railway station. There, Anton Graf was waiting. He accompanied me and several other Jewish people to Katowice, where he had found us our new employers. Mine were a married couple, Maria and Eberhard Borowski (Anton was their family friend). He told them I was a Polish Catholic country girl. They had no idea who I really was. Maria Borowski was waiting for me at the Katowice railway station. She was a very attractive Austrian woman; she had dark hair and blue eyes. Her husband, Eberhard Borowski (a Silesian German), was a lawyer and an officer in the German army. She was a spoiled woman, demanding and convinced of her right to demand.

"Their little boy, Radulf, was one and a half years old when I arrived; he was two and a half when I left. I got very attached to him. He was bright and mischievous, and I loved him. I slept in his room. I cooked and cleaned and did the grocery shopping and took care of little Radulf from early morning 'til late at night.

"When Eberhard would come home, his wife, Maria, would complain to him about me. She would tell him that I worked too slowly, and Eberhard would walk with me to the window, point to the Auschwitz chimneys in the distance, and say, 'If you don't work faster, I will send you there!'

"When Eberhard came home on leave, on Sundays he and his wife, Maria, would get up and get dressed, and they would announce that they were going for a walk and they expected a meal to be ready two hours later. Once there was nothing in the house except dry peas, beets, and potatoes. I made pea soup and cooked the beets and

grated them and made potato dumplings (*kupytka*). They
returned home, were pleased with the meal, and Maria did
not complain, so Auschwitz was pushed once again into
the ever-looming background.

"Once in a while Maria would have tea parties for her
lady friends (wives of officers). They would sip tea that I
served and eat cookies that I had baked. One day they were
discussing a hypothetical situation: how would each one
of them react, what would each one of them say and do, if
they had a Jew in the room. Their hatred, their cruelty, and
their lack of imagination were unparalleled. I kept serving
tea, pretending I was not listening to this surreal discussion!

"Once, while he was away, Eberhard sent a huge parcel to his wife. There were no handles to carry it. I was
to bring it home from the post office. As I was struggling with the parcel, I saw on the street an obviously
mentally handicapped young man pulling a wagon; he
said he would bring the parcel home, on the wagon, in
exchange for 15 marks. The superintendent helped me
carry it upstairs.

"At the time, Maria's mother was visiting from Vienna.
She asked me how I had managed to bring the parcel home;
I told her. Both Maria and her mother started yelling at me:
How did I dare spend money on this?! I had two pockets
in my apron, one for Maria's money and one for my own
money; I said I would put 15 marks from my own pocket
into Maria's pocket. They kept yelling, 'How do you, a
Polish woman, dare give work to a German man?!' I replied,

'I did a good deed; I, a Pole, gave work to a weak-minded German person who was standing idly on the street!'"

I can imagine the scene, her outrage. She just had to stand up to those two women, even if it meant risking her life.

"In the evenings, Maria would come to the kitchen to talk with me. Our kitchen conversations were interesting and dangerous. One evening she came and announced, 'The Russians are in Reichenau-Rzeszów. What would you do if you were a German?' I replied with conviction, 'Hitler is not going to let the Russians win!'

"Another evening Maria arrived quite shaken. 'Ola, there was an attempt to kill Hitler!' I answered, 'But I bet he's alive!' 'Yes,' she responded, and I continued, 'I always say, "Nothing will ever happen to him. He is a very strong man."'" Maria insisted, 'But the attempt to assassinate him!' And I concluded, 'Well, strong men always encounter opposition!'

"I was thirty-two, and so was Maria. She would repeat every word of mine to her husband, Eberhard, over the phone! I had to be mindful of my words.

"I would get packages from your father, from the Oflag, through Janek Kosiński (he was your father's friend, a Christian, and he too was a prisoner)." This was a way to ensure that people would not suspect my mother of being Jewish as in the Oflag everyone knew that my father was a Jew.

"One Sunday, I was writing a letter to Flora. I was sitting in the kitchen. An aunt who was visiting the family said, 'Come sit in Radulf's room and continue writing.' She remarked with some surprise, 'Oh! You write quickly, fluently.' 'Yes, I know how to write.' 'What about your parents, who were they?' 'They were bright.' These conversations were risky and I chose every word carefully.

"I was learning to speak German. Maria was trying to help, to explain some ideas. One evening she tried to explain what *seele* meant. 'Is it *animus* in Latin?' I asked. In her letters to her family and friends in Austria, Maria wrote about her Latin speaking, country-girl maid. Everyone found it hilarious."

After the war, my mother found Anton Graf's family in Germany. "I found out that Anton," the man who arranged her employment with Maria and Eberhard Borowski, "had never told his family what he had done during the war. He never told them how he saved Jews. Perhaps he did not want them to resent how he had endangered their lives. Perhaps he was not someone who dwelt on the past. I tried to get him to be on the list of the Righteous Ones at Yad Vashem. I could not find others who were saved by him. I tried.

"Many years later, a long time after the war, I got the Borowskis' address in Vienna from Anton Graf's family in Germany. The two families had remained in touch after the war. I wrote to Maria Borowski, told her the truth, that I was Jewish. She never replied to my letter."

Factory Worker

"ANTON GRAF HAD ARRANGED FOR ME TO BE A maid in the Borowskis' household and for Flora, called Wala (Waleria Kosieracka), to be a maid in Bytom (Beuthen).

"Flora worked for a nice German family, the Sigel family. He was the director of heavy industry in Silesia. Flora had her own room at the Sigel family's home. She had to clean and cook and help the children with their homework. When the assignment was particularly challenging, the children would be told, 'With this type of question, go ask Wala!'

"In 1944, when the order came that all Poles working for Germans must go to work in the mines, Mr. Sigel arranged for Flora and me to work together in an ammunitions factory.

The Lignoza managers were upset with the two Polish women who did not greet them and could not work in the lab,"—I do not really know what this means, and I did not ask when I could have—"so I went to work at a press. It was extremely hot there.

"I was the one dealing with Herr Dudek. He refused to speak in Polish; he was a *Volksdeutsche*, as were most of the Silesian Poles. I would go into his office and say in Polish, '*Ja mam ważną sprawę do załatwienia i będę mówiła po polsku, a Pan może odpowiadać po niemiecku.*' (I have an important matter to discuss with you; I will talk in Polish, and you, sir, can answer in German.)

"The other women workers called me 'Our Lady' (*Nasza Pani*) since I addressed each as Madam (*Pani*)." My mother's 'formal' behaviour, her cool distance; she used all available strategies (linguistic and gestural) to make sure that those around her (except for her close family) were held at a distance. Sometimes it was perceived as aloofness, sometimes as elegance, and frequently as snobbery. She did not often feel immediate warmth toward anyone. She suspected people of being selfish, greedy, self-serving, dishonest. And she was often right.

"Things were changing fast. I was invited one last time for a Christmas lunch at Maria Borowski's home. She invited me along with my 'cousin Wala' (my sister Flora).

"When Flora and I were in Altberun (*Stary Bieruń*) in Silesia (*na Śląsku*), we lived in a work camp. There was a dining area where a woman cooked meals for the workers

We got the labourers' menu. The higher ranked workers were served better meals. Sometimes the cook would offer us some of the better, more nourishing dishes.

"Toward the end of 1944, the Germans were starting to feel less confident of their victory. They were starting to run away; they became rather humble. Whereas they had never said 'hello' to Flora and me before, now they were actually greeting us!

"At the work camp they organized a pig roast to bid goodbye to all those Germans who were leaving. The cook was told that the two Polish women were allowed to join. Flora and I came to the meal. We had always been ignored before, but this time it was different; they were making an effort to be civil. During the meal, the chief engineer asked us whether the food was to our liking; we were both stunned. We thanked him. We never saw this man again. He ran away with all the other Germans."

On the Run

"AFTER THIS EVENT, THINGS STARTED CHANGING even faster. The cook came to talk to us. She said that the Russians were bombing all possible targets and the ammunitions factory, filled with explosives, could be bombed at any minute. The cook suggested we run with her to the forest, to the mill. The Russians were coming. We ran; about one kilometre separated us from them! Since it turned out that we could not sleep at the mill, we ran to a tiny town where a co-worker of mine lived. We could stay there for a few days.

"The Germans were gone. We awaited the arrival of the Russians. The Russians were said to be walking through towns and villages and shooting.

"My sister declared that she would hug the first Russian who would show up. We told the young women in the house to hide; they were terrified of being raped.

"When someone knocked on the door, my sister and I, the only ones who spoke Russian fluently, went to open the door. In front of us stood a huge man with an enormous moustache. Icicles were hanging from his moustache. He was holding a gun. Flora certainly did not hug him; we lied and told him that a few old people lived in the house.

"He left, but others kept arriving at the door. Those were the frontline Russians. Mostly young criminals. Some quite charming. Stories of rape were circulating. The young women living in the house wanted me to open the door. The fact that I could communicate with those 'liberating' us made them feel safe.

"At this point I got a very high fever and was violently sick. Luckily two Jewish Russian officers came knocking on the door. They were intelligent men, and one of them was a medical doctor. They advised us to stay put, to wait. They said they would come to get us.

"Two weeks earlier I had received the last letter from your father from the Oflag. He wrote to say that we would be meeting in Łódź, our hometown.

"Flora and I did not have the patience to wait for the return of the Russian officers. We bought some *wódka*, and on January 31 we left. Whenever we wanted a ride, we would show the *wódka* and they would take us. We went through Częstochowa and Kraków. I was carrying a back-pack. Flora did not carry anything.

"Suddenly, unexpectedly, I heard someone calling me by my real name, 'Stefa!' I froze. I did not turn around. I was afraid this was blackmail. All those years of living in fear that my identity would be discovered. Instead, it was a friend from our high school, Dusia K.; she, her husband, and her child lived on the outskirts of Kraków. Flora and I spent a few days there.

"When we left, we stopped at a diner to eat lunch. Some Russian officers were there. They wanted to 'sleep' with me. They said, 'You slept with the Germans—the proof is that you are alive, so now....' Flora and I ran out through the back door (a waitress showed us the way)."

Łódź

"AN EXTREMELY SLOW TRAIN, MORE RIDES (thanks to the *wódka*), more 'on-the-road' adventures. We arrived in Łódź on February 17."

Three days after Valentine's Day. I don't think they had ever heard of such a holiday, and the thought of how Valentine's would have sounded in the context of the hell from which they were emerging makes me grimace. My mother arrived in Łódź eleven days before my father's thirty-fifth birthday. She was almost thirty-four years old.

"As we arrived in Łódź we headed straight to the house where we used to live. I asked if anyone had come and left a message for me. The superintendent (*dozorca*) asked us whether we had a father who had just returned from prison. I said, 'No'; I explained I had a husband. This question ought to have prepared me as to how your father, Marian, was going to look.

"The superintendent went to fetch the message and brought back a little card with Marian's distinct, beautiful handwriting: 'I am on Kruglańska,' followed by an address. Flora and I ran to Kruglańska. We arrived out of breath and excited, looking forward to this reunion. We were told that, indeed, Marian lived there, but he was at work! He was working?! Where? In the militia? Why?!

"It turned out that Marian was one of the first ones to return from a prison camp to Łódź. We found out that every officer returning from a military prison camp had to either go to the front (as the Russian army was making its way to Berlin) or stay and serve in the militia.

"We went to the police station (*komisariat*), and we were told that Marian was driving from another station and would be arriving shortly at the station where we were waiting.

"He arrived. Unrecognizable. Aged. His eyes, lifeless."

She stops here. Her story ends here. Abruptly. My notes come to a sudden halt. Once she is reunited with my father, the story ends.

Postlude

AM I RELIEVED THAT HER STORY HAS ENDED? Am I disappointed? Am I surprised, having listened to it one last time, having translated it from Polish into English, and, finally, having told the story in her voice and in mine, in her voice through mine, that I have survived? Her words did not burn through me as I had feared; the desperate cruelty of the story did not demolish me as I was convinced it would.

I promised her that I would tell the story. Have I proven worthy of her trust? Would she have been satisfied with this account? How do I feel now about this story which has dominated my entire life? By telling it, have I managed to appease both of our souls? These questions, along with all my others, will forever remain unanswered. I have waited too long.

A few years ago, during a visit to Israel, some friends took me on a trip to Jerusalem. On the way, we stopped at the Soreq Caves. My friends wanted to visit the caves. The idea of caverns and grottos has never seemed particularly attractive to me. Their darkness and hollowness oppressed me. So I agreed most reluctantly.

As soon as I entered the caves, a mysterious darkness engulfed me. There was no backing out. I had to advance on the meandering path. As the entrance got farther and farther behind me, the darkness got thicker and closed in on me with its cold, sweaty clasp. I kept on advancing into this darkness. Gradually, slowly, the darkness dissipated. The caves were revealing their treasures: imposing and statuesque stalactites and stalagmites appeared, glowing in a dim, golden light. As I advanced, the caves became progressively more luminous; I was dazzled.

A while after this visit to the Soreq Caves, back in Halifax, I sat down at my kitchen table to paint three abstract images that would become *Golden Caves*. On my right, the large kitchen window overlooking the snow-covered garden was letting in a gentle light.

I chose a thick watercolour paper, took a large brush, and wet the paper. Then I loaded a round brush with

Holbein sepia, and instantly, heavy, quasi-black spec-
tres of stalactites and stalagmites appeared. With a large
bamboo pen I scratched the paper in vertical and diag-
onal lines. It seemed, then, essential that some of the lines
be twinned. Those very strong lines—sometimes single,
sometimes double—were structuring the entire painting.
I added some Winsor & Newton cadmium red hue, and
the entire picture appeared to be on fire. But I already
knew that this black and red hell contained a precious
treasure waiting to be revealed. And so I added quinacridone gold to the picture: a promise of things to come.
Yet, at this stage, the sepia darkness was dominant and
the spatter of sepia on the right side of the picture added
to the feeling of ashes rising. This picture was to become
Golden Caves I.

In the second painting, there were no more twinned
or single lines. Some remnants of the dark sepia formed
a semicircle, though the darkness was definitely receding.
Some cadmium red and the miraculous, luminous Winsor
& Newton transparent yellow, as well as an iridescent
medium and a more prominent quinacridone gold. Cool
Holbein's turquoise blue put out the fire. Finally came the
spraying of the top of the painting, tilting it so that all the
pigments could freely flow, all rigidity gone.

In a burst of colour, *Golden Caves III* was born, wet on
wet, with layers of drips, transparent yellow, Winsor &
Newton orange, and cooler but nonetheless outrageous
turquoise blue and Winsor & Newton's quinacridone

magenta. The darkness was chased away, gone; in an explosion of live joy, the treasure was revealed.

＊━━◇━◇━＊━

These three watercolours, in their progression from darkness to light, were, I think, my necessary prelude to the telling of this story.

Painting helped me to realize my courage. I felt that, for the process to be complete, I had to make the entire manuscript available to my children, for them to become her listeners and mine.

When they were little and then adolescents, I wanted to shield them from the harshness of the story. I feared that they were too vulnerable. Now they were sensitive and thoughtful adults, they were ready for the story, and it was time to pass it on.

I wrote to them, attached the manuscript, and invited them to read it. I clarified that it was an invitation, that they were free to decline. I invited them, if they wished, to jot down their thoughts on the impact that this story, untold until now, had on them.

Then I waited, wondering whether they would read it and how they would read it. Wondering which wounds I may have opened or reopened. Wondering what I may have stirred up. Worrying that I was disrupting their peace. Worrying that I was asking for too much. After all, this was an invitation to face their monsters.

The answers arrived—some quickly, others after a few months. Moving, brave, and generous. They listened and responded with open hearts. They shared all this wealth they carry within them. Their wealth of vulnerability, suffering, and compassion. Their wealth of humanity. All four wrote, and it was, once again, my turn to listen.

"…I feel so deeply appreciative that you wrote this and so honoured and touched and amazed that you dedicated it to us the way you did…."

"This is an incredible thing you have done…with her and for us and, when the time is right, for all the people who will get to experience this in their own ways."

"Reading it, knowing that it is written, understanding some of what formed you, gave me some relief (which I hadn't expected)."

"How has your trauma, as passed to you from your mother, been passed to me? I have been rolling and rerolling this question in my mind for months now. I started just before I read your manuscript. And after I read your manuscript, which gave firmness to my theories, I kept rolling the question until it was so long and so thin that it could stand as its own fresh neural pathway in my head."

"As I opened your document, I kind of went into it thinking I already knew these stories, heard them straight from your own mother's mouth, only to realize how little I'd actually heard, and to realize how much you had. To listen to you now channel the voice of the monster you'd hoped to transmute into something good in me and my siblings. When I reached the postlude, I put my face in my hands and sobbed. Maybe some part of me really did painfully know all of this insanity all along. Then I cried—how you painted your way into and out of the caves."

"I came home. I tried to go to bed. I sweated through my clothes, became insatiably thirsty, stood up, lay down, paced from room to room with terror and incapacity, my mind in utter panic. I got in and out of the bath. Another glass of water. Laboured breathing. After the worst of the physical and mental unhinged chaos, I arrived at the clarity. That I was, in fact, outright repeating some of my grandmother's stories."

I was devastated. What had I unleashed? What had I provoked? I spent a few restless and sleepless nights. I apologized.

"I feel reading the book was a big bite of apple…the apple consumed me….Rereading now. Incredible. So grateful for your rising to the challenge; you have refined in this document a powerful expression of your spirit."

"I feel like puzzle pieces that have existed for a long time are somehow emotionally fitting together. I remember being a little kid and asking, 'How did they all die?' and I remember being gently told (just that first time) that I could hear more about it when I was older, so while not much was said on that occasion, something transmitted in that moment made a lasting impression. Later on, of course, there were more conversations about it. I also remember a picture I drew as a kid, a sketch of people burnt in the ovens. I don't know what happened to that picture, but I remember how it looked."

I too remember the picture. And the sharp pang of pain and guilt I experienced when this child showed it to me. I still remember the black and brown lines on the cheap, yellowish paper. And already then, a glimpse of the unwelcome truth: the transmission that I so feared was inescapable. That day I should have realized that those Nazi incineration ovens will stay present in me and my children until our deaths.

"…the book was the most amazing thing I have ever read; reading it shook me deeply.…"

"I cannot say how the stories you did not tell me (in words) shaped me, because I am unsure as to whether I still 'heard' them by other means. Did their untold-ness in words make them more powerful, because their transmission was more implicit and subconscious?"

"Over time, I became more aware (even if only implicitly) that this story did exist, and that our compassion usually cannot depend on understanding the person's background, because we never really know their background.…"

"With your mother, my grandmother, perhaps I had the choice to listen precisely because you had none. When she'd end a story tersely with '*coś okropnego*' ('just horrible'), she was shouldering the pain for me. And when she'd conclude sweetly with '*rozumiesz?*' ('you understand?'), she was telling me she adored me no matter how poorly I listened. Now I wonder if she could afford to because long ago she'd already primed you as her chosen listener."

"You ask how my listening to this untold story has affected me; so much self-doubt has been cultivated about your own ability to tell this story correctly, and it seems, already having a similar psyche to you, that I modelled my own crippling self-criticism in life on these anciently retransmitted wounds of the universe; your story here retills this land with profound humanity. Perhaps now, remembering my grandmother's oft-repeated expression to me, '*Zobaczymy co z Ciebie wyniknie*' ('We'll see what becomes of you'), I can recognize these haunting wounds—hers, yours, and mine—and listen beyond."

So did I, after all, manage to protect my children from her frustration and her anger? I doubt it more and more. Yet how could I have been so pitifully, so distressingly, so self-servingly naive to believe that I could protect my children from the story, from its insanity?

"We sometimes partition our lives into 'before' an event and 'after' an event, because it transforms the way we understand ourselves and our world. Reading the manuscript was such an event: those pivotal elements are not necessarily in any of the Holocaust-related facts, rather they are somewhere in the telling of the story."

One of my children had been with me beside my mother when she drew her last breath.

"I remember watching her last exhalation. For years afterward, I would rehearse this final event, in solitude. Often rehearsing it as I lay in bed before going to sleep, actually physicalizing the gesture in my own body, a strange lullaby, trying to make sense of this transformative gift: diaphragm suddenly contracting, back curving into a hunch, neck outstretching, mouth and lips rounding out, and lungs' last emptying."

Will all those voices—my mother's and mine, mine and my children's—will they quiet down? Will the din subside? Will all this telling and retelling, all this listening, bring about some temporary peace? To my children? To me?

One of my children referred to "the many-decades-long shock wave which left us standing as we are today. Hurt."

I have often dreamt of a magical operation which would metamorphose all this suffering into beauty and praise, soulfulness and joy. I think of Baudelaire's poem, "L'Invitation au voyage," and especially its refrain:

Là, tout n'est qu'ordre et beauté,
Luxe, calme et volupté.

I dream that the rest of the journey—mine, my children's, and their children's—will be a journey of peace, order, and beauty. I dream for our journey to be nothing but calm and harmony.

By telling this story, I have conquered my overwhelming fear of it. By telling it, I have gotten rid of some of the self-loathing which was entangled in it. The story, transformed by its telling, will continue to live in me 'til the day I die.

By painting my way into and out of the caves, by finally telling her story and mine, I have found in that hollow place within me tenderness and compassion. By telling it, I hope to have lifted some of the shadows, to have brought in some light.

I am grateful to my mother for her generosity in bringing me into the world, grateful for this amazing gift of life, and grateful for this story of despair and survival, her resilience and mine. Against all odds.

Halifax, Nova Scotia
November 2018

The Uses of Sorrow
 by Mary Oliver

(In my sleep I dreamed this poem)

Someone I loved once gave me
a box of darkness.

It took me years to understand
that this, too, was a gift.

Glossary

akcja (declension: *akcje*) (Polish): Operation.

Arbeitskarte (German): An ID issued during World War II by workplaces in occupied Poland.

Armia Krajowa (*A.K.*) (Polish): "The Home Army." During World War II, the Home Army was the leading resistance organization within the Polish underground movements.

Armia Ludowa (*A.L.*) (Polish): Literally "People's Army." An army set up by the Communist Polish Workers' Party during World War II.

Galey Tsahal (Hebrew): The Israel Defence Forces radio channel.

Gestapo (German): Abbreviation of *Geheime Staatspolizei* (Secret State Police in English). The official secret police of Nazi Germany and German-occupied Europe.

godzina policyjna (Polish): Literally "Police hour"; curfew. A regulation requiring people to be off the streets and in their homes, often between 8:00 p.m. and 6:00 a.m.

Gwiazda Dawida (Polish): Star of David. See *Magen David*.

Hotel Polski (Polish): Polish Hotel. A hotel in Warsaw located
at 29 Długa Street. In 1943, the hotel was used by Germans
as an internment place for Jews. Many historians see the
Hotel Polski affair as a German trap to lure the richer
Jews out of their hiding places in Warsaw, under false
pretenses, and steal their possessions while sending them to
extermination camps.

kenkarta (Polish), *Kennkarte* (German): ID card.

Magen David (Hebrew): David's shield. See *Gwiazda Dawida*.

matka (*mama*, *mamusia*) (Polish): Mother.

Nazi incineration ovens: Where the bodies of those murdered
(e.g., by gassing) were disposed of.

Offizierslager (abbreviation: *Oflag*) (German): "Officers' camp."
A prisoner-of-war camp for officers captured by the
German army during World War II. Honouring the Geneva
Convention (1929), the Nazis did not murder the officers
imprisoned in these Oflags (including the minority of
Jewish officers among them).

Ojcze Nasz (Polish): Our Father.... The beginning of the Lord's
Prayer.

Pan, Pani (Polish): Pan and Pani are the basic honorific styles
used in Polish to refer to a man or woman respectively.

Reich (German): Literally "Realm." With new territories
annexed into the German state's administration, the
nation was renamed the Great German Reich. From
January 1933 to May 1945, Hitler's regime was designated
as the Third Reich.

Righteous Ones (Righteous Among the Nations): A title used
by Yad Vashem (Israel) to recognize and honour those

non-Jews who risked their lives during the Holocaust to
save Jews from extermination by the Nazis.

Skull Chapel (*Kaplica Czaszek*): The Skull Chapel in Czermna is
located in one of the oldest villages in Poland, near Kudowa-
Zdrój. The Chapel was built in 1776 and is a mass grave.

'Soap': During World War II it was believed that soap was
being mass produced from the bodies of the victims of Nazi
concentration camps located in German-occupied Poland.
The Yad Vashem Memorial has stated that the Nazis did
not produce soap from Jewish corpses on an industrial scale.
Rumours that soap from human corpses was mass produced
and distributed were deliberately used by the Nazis to
frighten camp inmates.

Spielberg Foundation: Organization that filmed the
testimonies of nearly 52,000 survivors of the Holocaust.

Transport Führer (German): Transport Leader. Officer in
charge of transport.

Trzynastka (Polish): Number 13. The Group Thirteen network was
a Jewish collaborationist organization in the Warsaw Ghetto.
The unit reported directly to the German Gestapo office.

Umschlagplatz (German): The "collection point" or "reloading
point" were areas adjacent to railway stations in occupied
Poland, where Jews were assembled from the ghettos,
crowded onto freight cars, and deported to Nazi death camps.

the underground: Resistance movements. See also *Armia
Krajowa (A.K.)*

Volksdeutsche (German): A Nazi concept to unite its race/
people; referred to ethnic Germans living outside of
Germany and Austria who did not necessarily possess
German or Austrian citizenship.

Yad Vashem (Hebrew): The World Holocaust Remembrance
   Center, Israel's official memorial to the victims and
   the heroes of the Holocaust. Yad Vashem, the Shoah
   Remembrance Authority, was established in 1953 by the
   Israeli parliament.
Yom Kippur (Hebrew): Day of Atonement. The holiest day of
   the year in Judaism.

Dramatis Personae

Andrzej: A young boy who lived with his family in an apartment above the narrator (as a child).

Ania: Sister of Hanka Klein's husband.

Anton Graf: Transport Führer, German officer; helped save Jewish people; placed Stefa and Flora with Austrian and German families.

Bogdański family: The owners of the place in Milanówek where Sonia was hiding (under a false name) and where she died.

Celina: Stefa's friend; was in the Warsaw Ghetto; her husband was a Jewish officer in the same Oflag as Marian. Celina escaped from the Ghetto and hid on the Aryan side; she survived the war.

Dorota: An acquaintance of Stefa's in the Warsaw Ghetto; helped her elderly parents commit suicide; survived the Holocaust and ended up as a patient in an asylum.

Dudek (Herr): A *Volksdeutsche*; worked for the Lignoza ammunitions factory where Stefa and Flora worked.

Dusia: Stefa's high school friend (from Łódź); during the war lived on the outskirts of Kraków.

Eberhard: A lawyer and an officer in the German army; his wife was Maria Borowski. Stefa was a maid in his household.

Edek: A Jewish man who worked for the Leszno 13 office. Having survived the war, he immigrated to Israel and became a model Israeli citizen.

Eliasz: A distant relative of Sonia's; gave Stefa the money to pay her way out of the Ghetto.

Eliza: She and her sister Aniela lived in the Ghetto in the same apartment with Sonia, Flora, and Stefa.

Felek: A Jewish lawyer; was in the Warsaw Ghetto, survived, and practised law in Paris after the war.

Flora: Stefa's sister. Her false name was Waleria Kosieracka (Wala).

Hala: Flora and Stefa's friend in Poland and afterward in Israel.

Hanka: Flora and Stefa's cousin; survived the war and lived in France after the war.

Itzhak: Sonia's relative; was a known Yiddish and Hebrew poet; was gassed.

Jaga: Flora's friend; a devout Catholic; later became a nun.

Janek: A Christian friend of Marian's in the Oflag; helped Stefa and Marian exchange letters and packages.

Janina: Wife of Zygmunt Kostro; mother of Teresa Kostro; grandmother of Róża and Piotr.

Jasia: A Jewish woman; belonged to a network and saved Jews; connected Stefa to the German Anton Graf; was later executed by Poles.

Jędrek: Niusia and Jerzy's son (Niusia was Hanka's sister).

Jerzy: Niusia's husband; Jędrek's father.

Jurek: Friend of Stefa and Marian.

Lusia: Mietek's wife; Hanka's sister-in-law.

Maks: Worked for the office at Leszno 13 (*Trzynastka*);
    survived the war and later immigrated to Israel.

Maria: Eberhard Borowski's wife. Stefa was her maid and her
    son Radulf's nanny.

Marian: Stefa's husband; survived the war in an Oflag.

Marta: A lawyer.

Mietek: Brother of Hanka and Niusia; Lusia's husband; wrote
    poetry in Hebrew; perished in Auschwitz.

Mirka: Mother of Hanka, Niusia, and Mietek. Mirka's false
    name was Antonina. Stefa lived with her for a while.

Niusia: Stefa's relative; Hanka and Mietek's sister.

Piotr (Piotruś): Stefa and Marian's stillborn son.

Radulf: Son of Maria and Eberhard Borowski. Stefa was his
    nanny.

Róża: Daughter of Teresa Kostro; granddaughter of Janina and
    Zygmunt Kostro.

Schumann (Pani): A *Volksdeutsche*; hired Flora to be her
    children's nanny.

Sigel family: A German family. Anton Graf helped Flora to be
    hired as a maid for the family.

Sonia (Zofia Knopf): Stefa's mother. Her false name was
    Franciszka Wolańska.

Stefa (Stefania Knopf): Sonia's daughter; Flora's sister;
    Marian's wife. Her false name was Aleksandra Karpińska
    (Ola).

Strikman (Robert): A director in the office at Nowy Świat 68.

Tadek: Son of Hanka's maid, Anna; a denunciator, a
    blackmailer.
Tammy: An Israeli childhood friend of the narrator.
Teo: Flora's husband; was in the Oflag with Marian.
Zygmunt: Janina Kostro's husband; a Pole, a Catholic, a lawyer,
    and bailiff in the Warsaw Ghetto; helped Stefa and Flora.

Use of Names, Nicknames, and Initials

I have provided some authentic first names and sometimes
last names as well. I did that whenever I could obtain the
permission of the surviving children or grandchildren of the
persons mentioned. Below is the list, in alphabetical order, of
the authentic names (true and assumed for survival purposes)
used in the text:

    Eliasz R.
    Flora (Waleria Kosieracka, Wala)
    Hala L.
    Itzhak K.
    Jaga N.
    Janina Kostro
    Marian
    Piotr (Piotruś)
    Stefania (Stefa, Aleksandra Karpińska, Ola)
    Teresa Kostro
    Zofia Knopf (Sonia, Franciszka Wolańska)
    Zygmunt Kostro

All the other names in the text are pseudonyms. Coming
up with the pseudonyms turned out to be a complex, albeit

fascinating, task as I wished to preserve the specific flavour of each name.

Moreover, my mother referred to some people by their nickname (a very common practice in Polish), to some by their full given name, and to many by their last name. When a relationship evolved, a person first referred to by their family name was later referred to by their given name. I tried to reflect that in my text.

Acknowledgements

My deepest gratitude to my husband for having allowed me the space to write and to my children, Sageev, Jasmine, Daniel, and Jonathan, for being the incredible people they are, for their support, for their trust, and for having contributed with such depth and generosity to the postlude. This text would not have been the same without their contribution. To Dani, for the steady and inspired accompaniment, and for believing in me. To Bruce, Sean, Kelly, Marionne, Duncan, Morgan, Melissa, John, Nadine, Julia, and the entire team at U of R Press, my immense appreciation, and to Jan for pointing the manuscript in the right direction. To Henny, for the meticulous typing and patient copyediting—through endless versions. To Clare, for her selfless and brilliant reading and editing. Thank you all for being there, for being my listeners, and for making me feel less alone. Thanks to all those who, along the way, helped with various aspects of this work: Andrea, Krysia, Mati, Monika, Róża, and many, many others.

About the Author

Born in Łódź, Poland, Irene Oore immigrated to Israel with her parents at eight years old. There, she went to a French convent in Jaffa (Pensionnat Saint-Joseph) and subsequently studied literature at the University of Tel Aviv. She later obtained her doctorate from the Univeristy of Western Ontario and is currently a professor of French and Quebec literature at Dalhousie University, Halifax. Irene loves her family, her children and grandchildren, reading and writing, gardening, and painting water-colours. Her paintings have been shown in exhibitions and published in journals.

A Note About the Type

This book is set in Adobe Caslon. Based on a long running serif font first designed by William Caslon in 1722 and used extensively throughout the British Empire in the early eighteenth century, Adobe Caslon was designed by Carol Twombly, who studied specimen pages printed by Caslon between 1734 and 1770 for this revival. Used widely in the early days of the American Colonies and the font used for both the US Declaration of Independence and Constitution, Caslon is generally considered to be among the world's most "user-friendly" typefaces.

The Regina Collection

Named as a tribute to Saskatchewan's capital city with its rich history of boundary-defying innovation, *The Regina Collection* builds upon University of Regina Press's motto of "a voice for many peoples." Intimate in size and beautifully packaged, these books aim to tell the stories of those who have been caught up in social and political circumstances beyond their control.

To see other books in *The Regina Collection*
visit www.uofrpress.ca

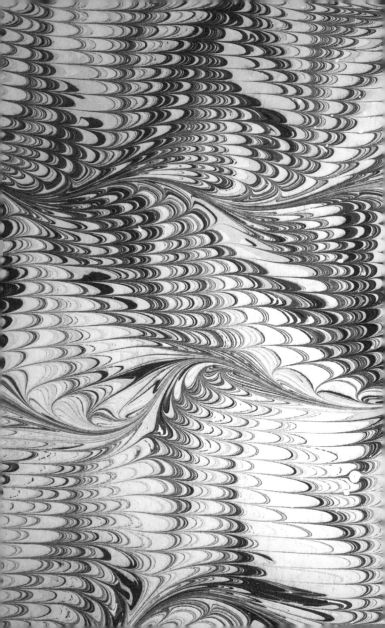